HALLELUJAH! PASS THE GRITS

Danny Key

Righter Books

WINGATE UNIVERSITY LIBRARY

Copyright 2008 by Danny Key
All rights reserved

No portion of this work may be reproduced
without prior written permission from the
author.

Righter Publishing Company, Inc.
PO Box 105
Timberlake, North Carolina 27583

www.righterbooks.com

First Edition
August, 2008

Printed and bound in the United States of
America

Library of Congress Control Number
2008932997

ISBN: 978-1-934936-10-8
Hallelujah! Pass the Grits
By Danny Key

Author's Preface

If you are looking for a great piece of literature to read then put this book down. I am not a great writer. I am, however, a pretty good story teller.

This is a collection of stories I heard growing up along with personal commentary on life in a small southern mill town. I make fun of a lot of things, but mostly I make fun of myself. These stories are fact, fun, fiction, and fantasy all rolled into one big mess.

Some things in life happen to you that appear to be ordinary but a little exaggeration of the circumstances here and there, you have a funny story to share. That is what story tellers do.

The some of the commentary is my ranting and raving about the silliness of some of the ideas and philosophies that prevail in my beloved South. Don't get me wrong, I love the South and would not want to live anywhere else. But I find some things about our lifestyle unusual and funny.

Sit back and enjoy. Maybe you'll get a laugh or two and a story to share with a friend.

Dedication

This book is dedicated to my wonderful friends at the National Association of College Stores in Oberlin, Ohio. Over the years they have put up with my "southernisms."

I owe a debt to my crazy relatives whose adventures gave me a reason to write. Thanks for being weird! Who wants to read about normal people?

A special thanks to the College Store Association of North Carolina and South Carolina for their encouragement to write this.

To my mom I give special thanks for being an example of what a perfect parent is like. Your love is the strongest anchor in the universe.

To Melvin, who puts up with my wild imagination and goofy view of life every day of his patient life, there are no words to express my gratitude.

And to the wonderful people who are blessed to live in the South, I love you! And, *Bless Your Big Ole Southern Heart!*

Changeless Southern Women

My grandmother's yard had two giant live oak trees. Their branches spread out over half of her property and their roots were above ground. They were my childhood playground.

All sorts of activity took place under those trees. My grandmother would sit in the wooden swing and shell peas, string beans, or peel peaches for hours on end. All the neighborhood women would be around her, each of them busy with some sort of household chore they had brought with them. This was the gathering place to exchange information, and who better to do that than my grandmother.

My grandmother knew everybody in town and everything about them. She was so "interested" in other people's lives that she kept a party line telephone until the phone company did away with them.

You could learn who was sick and what they were sick with, whose husband was caught doing something nasty with another woman, why the preacher's wife wore dresses made of flour sacks, and whose children were growing up to be a disappointment to their parents.

As a child, I spent thousands of hours at my grandmother's house playing under those same trees while the women worked and talked. I learned a lot from my eavesdropping, most of which I repeated to anyone who would listen. My mother was my most avid listener. The subject that created the most excitement among this group of women was something they called "the change."

If your knowledge regarding a subject comes from the discussions of genteel southern women sitting under a giant shade tree you are most likely to get a few things confused. To my eight-year-old brain, this thing they called "the change" was a horrible infliction that all women seemed destined to suffer once they got a certain age. I heard about Olive, who spent her days living under the kitchen sink; Susie, who talked to the man in the moon while standing in the backyard at night; Mabel, who shot her husband while he was sitting in the outhouse; and Artie Mae, who dyed her hair red and sold her children to her sister. According to my grandmother and her friends, all this weird behavior was due to "the change."

This information led me to the conclusion that my mother must never go through such a horrible illness. I had to come up with a plan to prevent this change from afflicting my family. I knew I had my work was cut out for me because, according to my grandmother's friends, there was nothing anyone could do to stop it.

Undaunted by any facts, I decided that if this "change" is truly inevitable, then I must hide all signs of it when my mom got it. I would crawl under the sink first so there would be no room for her. I would follow her outside at the first signs of a desire to talk to the man in the moon. I would keep sharp objects and razors away from her in case she decided to shave her head. I would search the bathroom for any signs of hair dye. If she decided to sell me, I would act like I was mentally ill so that no one else would want me.

I decided to make my plan known to my family while we were taking one of our Sunday afternoon car rides. I announced to my unsuspecting family that I had everything under control when the change attacks mom. Their reaction was extreme, to say the least. My father stopped the car, my mother turned sickly pale and my sister laughed hysterically. I had apparently broken some rule of social behavior by mentioning this subject out loud. After everybody regained their composure my mother politely told me that the change is a subject for grownups only and I could not possibly ever understand. After looking at me in disbelief, my dad started the car and we resumed our drive.

As the years passed, I learned that men in general do not understand this phenomenon and refuse to talk about it. This made the subject all the more fascinating to me. I soon discovered that there was another side to this change business—that it could be used as a

11

weapon or at least an excuse for doing silly things.

One time my mother drove all the way home from the A&P with the parking brake on.

When my father yelled at her, she replied, "Don't fuss at me! You know I am going through the change!"

This ended the conversation immediately. After this success, my mother used the change as an excuse several more times—when she wore two different shoes to church, when she lost my sister in the Sears and Roebuck, and when she served raw eggs that she thought she had boiled to perfection.

I would not shut up about this subject and it became a big embarrassment to my family.

My grandmother and her friends had endless stories about the change and they seemed to love discussing all the facets of the change of life. They even had home remedies that they shared. I learned that my own grandmother had taken some sort of shots while she was afflicted with this malady. My dad told me that those shots were nothing more than sugar water and the doctor gave them to my grandmother to shut her up about all her imaginary symptoms related to the change.

After a while the subject died away and I found something else to occupy my overactive imagination.

I remember the day I decided to let well enough alone. My mother had locked herself out of the house one night while Dad and I had gone hunting. When we came home Mom was sitting on the back door steps, freezing from the cold. Before my dad could say a word, my mom resorted to the "change" excuse.

"This is not my fault," she cried. "You know I am going through the change and cannot be held responsible for my actions!"

When we got inside my dad said, "About this change business—change if you want to change, I don't care. I give you five minutes to get it over with."

I glanced at the back of my mother's dress as she crawled under the kitchen sink.

The True Meaning of "Bless Your Heart"

I grew up hearing and using the expression, "Bless Your Heart." Almost everybody I know uses this phrase as a permanent part of their vocabulary. In recent years incorrect interpretations of the meaning of "bless your heart" have surfaced. Most of these misinterpretations have come from our Northern neighbors. My friends at the National Association of College Stores in Oberlin, Ohio think it means, "You are nice but dumb as a rock." Granted on occasion, it can mean that. But that is the exception rather than the rule. To really explain the meaning let me share a conversation I overheard at the grocery store several years ago.

I was checking out the produce when two ladies bumped into each other. They were obviously old friends and took a few minutes to catch up on the local news.

"Did you hear about Bill, the man who lives three houses down from me?"

"Why yes, I did. Wasn't that a tragedy! What caused the argument in the first place?"

"Well, Bills' neighbor, Ed, had this huge old tree whose branches hung way over into Bills' yard. Every fall most of the leaves from that tree would fall into Bills' yard. They were constantly arguing about that. Bill wanted Ed to cut the tree down or at least trim the limbs over his yard back but Ed absolutely refused. This went on for years and I guess that it built up in Bill until he could not take it anymore. They argued and Bill went into his house and came out with a ball bat and beat Ed to death with it right there in the street between their houses!"

"Oh, how awful. I was away visiting my sister in Richmond while all that was going on. I had heard bits and pieces of the story. Isn't it a shame that people cannot get along in this world? What happened then?"

"Well, Bill went to trial and was given twenty-five years in the penitentiary for manslaughter. But you know what? I hear that he writes to his mama every day, bless his heart."

Therein lies the true meaning of "bless your heart." It is that eternal hope that in all of us there still exists a little bit of good. No matter how despicable a person is, no matter what horrible thing they have done, we just want a little part of them to at least appear to be good. Now this is not to say that my friends in the north do not share this same desire. I'm sure they do but it is rarely expressed. A good example of this can be seen between my wonderful friend, Kathy Grace, from Philadelphia and myself.

If we were driving along one day and a car driven by an elderly lady pulled out in front of us, almost causing us to wreck, Kathy would say, "Where the hell did that old woman learn to drive?"

On the other hand, I would say, "Where the hell did that old woman learn to drive, bless her heart."

Kathy is a wonderful and caring woman whom I admire and love dearly but the different responses from us illustrate the meaning of bless your heart. I would yell at the old woman but would believe that her bad driving is not her fault. That is implied when I say, bless her heart.

Bless your heart serves as a cushion to criticism that we dish out. I am not saying that other parts of the country do not share our desire to see some good in everyone. They just haven't come up with a good an expression like bless your heart. I assume this is why they do not attempt to cushion the verbal blows they deliver. There is no doubt that most people deserve to be yelled at sometime in their life. I certainly have. It is just easier to take when you bless my heart after cussing me out. That tells me that you really don't hate me and believe that I am basically good, despite my failings. Doesn't everyone want to feel good about themselves? We, in the south, are just doing our part to bring about some mental healing to those poor souls that cause our blood pressures to escalate to the point of a stroke.

Personally, I say it a lot because I have this serious flaw in my personality. I am too forgiving. I forgive everyone of everything eventually. I can't hold a grudge no matter how hard I try. I really don't like this trait and wish I could be angry with some people forever. I start out determined to hate someone who has wronged me, but it just takes too much effort. Nobody else in my family has this faulty gene. If you wronged my father, you were marked for life; there was no getting back into his inner circle. My mother is the same way. My sister is a little less rigid and has a little more ability to forgive and forget. Then there is me, sappy, soft, gullible me. The "bless your heart" guy. The one who thanks you for tripping him up on the playground.

In an age of misguided morals, crooked politicians, senseless wars, environmental poisoning, nuclear proliferation, zealots who kill in the name of religion, neglected children, businesses without a conscience, and unrelenting national debt, I believe the world can use a few more "bless your heart" folks who still hold on to the belief that man can be better than he is.

When Chickens Come Home To Roost

One of the distinctive characteristics of southern families is the number of off-the-wall, eccentric characters that make up one's family tree. There is at least one in every family.

People have blamed the heat, humidity, the moonshine, food, or the popular, "I married my first cousin." But for whatever reason, there always exists the black sheep, the misfit who is a total embarrassment to all their relatives. They are the favorite topic of discussion at family reunions.

"Poor Uncle Joe. Did you hear about him riding the in back of his pickup truck, naked as a jaybird while his dog was driving? He passed in front of his ex-girlfriend's' house. She called the police and they hauled his crazy ass off to jail. You know, the part where they keep the prisoners who are a little 'touched' in the head."

In my family, we are blessed with lots of "Uncle Joes." Most people call them nut cases but we refer to them as "colorful." No one fits that description better than my great Aunt Mae.

Aunt Mae was a larger than life persona who made her own rules as she went along, totally disregarding all social mores. She collected husbands and then discarded them when they were no longer amusing. My grandmother was embarrassed by Mae but I found her fascinating. Anybody can follow rules but Mae made up her own rules in the days before women's lib. Unlike her siblings, Mae chose to live in the city most of her life, rejecting the small town of her birth.

Mae had a flair for the dramatic. At her mother's gravesite, she wailed and moaned so loudly no one could hear the minister. This aggravated my mother to no end, since Mae had never been close to her mother. In fact, she practically ignored her mother. At this graveside service, Mae carried on like a professional mourner from Biblical days, waving her hands and rocking back and forth. She put on quite a show. I thought it was a performance worthy of an Academy Award. When we were dismissed to our cars, it took four strong men to drag her away because she pretended to faint every five steps. I felt like clapping when she finally made it to the car, but my mother was watching me with that look that said, "Don't even think about it."

As Mae grew older she decided that living in the city was not the best thing for a single woman. So she set out in search of a new husband. She found a farmer who lived way out in the country, married him, and moved to the farm. This man lived so far out that he did not have inside plumbing. Instead he had, what we call in the South, a path to the outhouse.

Outhouses were holes dug deep with

20

roughshod buildings built over them. The interior consisted of wooden seats built over the hole. Out houses were built a distance from the main house for obvious reasons. Mae's new husband was considered wealthy because his outhouse had two seats! Personally, I never understood why you would need a two-seater out house. The activity that goes on in there is best done alone, not with a crowd. Who wants to do their business with somebody else sitting a few inches away? At any rate, there were two seats in Mae's new outhouse.

Mae's new husband had warned her that she should always use the seat on the right because one of his chickens had built a nest under the seat on the left. Having to use an outhouse to begin with was insulting to Mae but what other choice was there? Since she hated the outhouse she would usually wait until the very last minute and then make a mad dash down the path, arriving just in time. She was not looking forward to winter and nagged her new husband for an inside toilet. This was after she discovered that one of her "wifely" duties was to empty the chamber pot every morning.

A chamber pot was a big tin pot with a lid that you kept under your bed. If you did not want to go to the outhouse at night, or if it was raining or cold, you could use the chamber pot as your toilet. Naturally they had to be emptied and cleaned every morning, a duty that has to rank at the bottom of disgusting household duties.

Outhouses also attracted varmints like spiders, bugs, rats, and snakes so you had to be on the lookout for these creatures when you visited an out house. One warm summer day Mae was busy inside the house when a pain struck. With no time to waste she ran down the path. When she entered the outhouse she forgot which seat she was supposed to use. Was it the one on the right as you face the seats or vice-versa? With no time left to make the decision she jumped on the left seat. Sitting on its nest, minding its own business was her husband's favorite chicken. Apparently chickens don't like for a three-hundred pound woman to sit over their nests. The chicken reached up and pecked Mae hard right on her ass.

Mae jumped up and tore out of the outhouse, pants around her ankles, screaming, "Snake, snake! I've been bit by a snake!" She ran to the field where her husband was working leaving bits of her clothing behind her. Imagine her new husband's reaction when his new wife arrived, naked from the waist down, bending over and screaming for him to do something quick.

"I've been bit by a snake! Help me!" she cried "Suck out the poison like they do on television. Hurry, I'm in pain!"

Her husband ignored her and took off running towards the outhouse yelling, "If anything has happened to that chicken there will be hell to pay!"

The judge granted the divorce on the grounds of irreconcilable differences.

Revival and Revenge

My grandmother's best friend was named Holly. She lived close enough that my grandmother could walk to her house every day for their daily gossip fests. They were a perfect match, each one contributing some facts regarding the latest dirt they had uncovered.

On occasion I would accompany my grandmother to Holly's house. I loved going there because her house was full of all kinds of interesting bric-a-brac and collectibles. Her relatives sent her something from the places they visited and Holly displayed them proudly.

After Holly's husband died, she sold her house and moved into a mobile home. She was one of the first people I knew to own a mobile home. I thought they were the neatest contraptions on earth and I nagged my parents constantly to buy one so we could move it every week. It sounded like a good idea to me. But for some reason my parents insisted that living in a brick house was better than living in a trailer. I chalked it up to them having no sense of adventure.

Holly was a religious person who attended church faithfully. Once in a while she would get excited during a lively service and start shouting. Shouting in church was a natural part of religion in some country churches. People would often stand and wave their hands

25

or run up and down the aisles praising the Lord. I was told that the city churches looked down on this practice and that no one ever shouts in a city church.

"Dead," my father used to say. "Those cold city churches wouldn't know the Holy Ghost if He came down and slapped them."

Most of the older people in our church shouted at one time or another. You never saw any young people shouting. I thought it looked like fun and always tried to figure out when was the best time to shout and what you should say and was it better to stand still or run around?

I learned something interesting about shouting one evening while our family was driving home from a revival meeting. Holly had been quite active that night. She had shouted and thrown a hymnal or two.

My dad observed, "That was some meeting tonight. Miss Holly was sure caught up in the spirit."

"In the spirit my ass," my mother replied. "I know for a fact that Holly and the two women that she banged in the head with a hymn book have been arguing all week long. Mama told me all about it. She used her shouting spell as an opportunity to get revenge!"

"How can you say that?" my dad objected. "It could have been an accident."

"It was no accident," my mom replied. "Holly is a mean old biddy who gets even with people whatever way she can and tonight she used the Holy Ghost!"

What a brilliant idea," I thought. "Getting even with somebody by knocking them upside the head with a hymnbook while in church. You could claim that you were in the spirit and the odds of someone throwing one back at you were slim.

My admiration for Miss Holly grew by leaps and bounds. She had found the perfect way to pay someone back who had wronged her. As soon as we got home I went to my room and starting compiling my "Hallelujah Hit List."

Ten minutes later I finished my list. First on the list was David who told everyone that I was such a sissy that I probably squatted to pee. Second was Danny because he was a good athlete and made fun of me every time we played ball, leaving me to be chose dead last for any team. Next there was John who forged my name on a love letter to a girl in our Sunday school class who was always sneezing into her hand and then rubbing it into her hair.

Just wait until the next church service, I thought. As soon as Holly started to shout, I would fling hymnbooks at the guys on my list. But there was one flaw to my plan. I was no better at throwing hymnbooks than I was at throwing a baseball. I could hit *somebody* but I couldn't hit a selected individual. I thought about practicing but how does one go about asking the preacher to borrow a couple of hymnbooks to throw at home? I couldn't tell him why I wanted the books and I shouldn't lie to him. That would mean immediate and eternal punishment in Hell according to my parents.

I guess it was okay to call Miss Holly a hypocrite, but it was wrong to lie to the preacher. Then the perfect answer to my dilemma came to me. I would get Holly to throw the hymnbooks for me. All I needed to do was to go with my grandmother the next time she visited Holly and tell her that the boys on my list had been spreading ugly rumors about her. I got another inspiration that would remove me from the whole incident. I would tell my grandmother. Then she would tell Holly. At last, a fail proof plan for revenge.

"Grandma, did you know that some boys in my Sunday school class make fun of Miss Holly? David and Danny make fun of her lazy eye. They imitate her and tell people to stare at her eye. David even drew a picture of her in his Sunday school book and he only gave her one big eye. John thinks she is a witch who eats cat food. I heard him telling the girls in our class that her lazy eye came about because she was experimenting with evil spells and spilled some sort of potion on her hands and when she rubbed her eye, it caused it to droop. Is that true, Grandma?"

My grandmother listened carefully as I rambled on, never stopping to question the authenticity of my claims. I could see the wheels turning in her head and I knew that the next time she and Holly were together; my story would be related and probably exaggerated.

I couldn't wait until the next church service. Wanting to be near the action, I took a seat right in front of Holly. Then it happened. Halfway through the choir song Holly leaped to her feet, praising the Lord. I was tempted to turn around and hand her the hymn books, but instead I sat quietly waiting for her to take aim and let them fly. I could see the targets in my side vision. Suddenly a hymnbook slipped from Holly's hand and landed flat on the top of *my* head. The shock made me turn around just in time for one of her fingers to poke me right in the eye. My plan had gone badly awry.

The minister got up and announced his sermon title, "Vengeance is mine, I will repay, thus said the Lord."

Defining a Family

My mother put the telephone receiver back in place and stared at the phone for a few minutes. I saw her eyes moisten with tears. She got her coat and car keys and told me that she would be back in a few minutes. I knew better than to ask any questions. I had seen that look before. Sadness mingled with anger. It would be an hour before I discovered the source of her deep emotions.

When my mother returned, all of our lives changed. She brought with her a cute, perky, energetic blond-haired little girl with a smile that warmed an entire room. Her name was Patsy and she would become my new sister.

In reality Patsy was my first cousin. Her father was my dad's youngest brother. He was only married to her mother for a very short time before he joined the Army and was sent away to fight in World War II. When he returned from the war he acted like Patsy or her mother never existed. He had been courting another woman before he went overseas and when he returned to the states, he returned to her instead of Patsy's mother. Ironically this other woman lived a few blocks from Patsy and her mother.

The first time Patsy saw him was when he walked by her house on his way to his new

31

love's house. He didn't even look in Patsy's direction. Come to think of it, that would describe his whole relationship with her; he just never looked in her direction.

His second wife was the love of his life and they adored each other. Their daughter received all the attention and affection two parents could give. Being born to the woman he adored made her the rightful heir to his love and devotion. He showed this in a thousand ways with little regard or remorse as to how this affected my sister, Patsy.

I hated him for his negligence and coldhearted behavior. In his later years, he made a feeble attempt to make up for the past but he failed miserably. Try as he might, it was evident that he did not love Patsy and no manner of guilt or shame could change that fact.

His willingness to give Patsy up granted my family the privilege of having her in our lives. I fell for her instantly. She was everything I wasn't. She was outgoing, resourceful, outrageous, lively, cunning, worldly, and full of life. Our home was transformed by her presence and we loved her.

My dad had always had a special place in his heart for her and worried about her all the time. When she came to live with us, Dad seemed at peace. She was with him where he could watch over her, protect her, and try to make up for the love that her biological father refused to give her.

My mother adored her too and they bonded immediately. Mother never referred to her as her husband's niece but as her daughter.

Once in a while I would ask my mother to recall that night when she went to pick up Patsy. It never failed to get her blood boiling.

When my mother arrived at my uncle's house she found Patsy locked out and sitting on the front porch steps in the cold. Her clothing had been stuffed into a paper bag. She was scared, hurt, cold, and lonely. Coming upon that scene proved too much for my mother to bear. She went into a rage and beat on the front door until my uncle opened it. When he did, her contempt and anger boiled over and she let him have it with both barrels, castigating him for his cold-hearted cruelty.

I wasn't there and Patsy doesn't remember it, but my mother will never forget it. After my mother cursed him and his wife until they turned pale, she loaded Patsy into the car and came home. Mother vowed then and there that as long as she had breath in her body Patsy would have a loving home and family.

Thus began our lives as a family of four. I was proud to brag to everyone that I had a sister. This was confusing to my schoolteacher who was puzzled that my mother had given birth without anyone knowing she was pregnant. It took a some explaining by my parents because I went around telling everyone that my sister had arrived and she was 12 years old.

Patsy brought a whole new meaning of fun and laughter into my life. She challenged me to do things that I had been too scared to try. She teased me and coached me through my first crush, although she lamented the fact that I was too shy. We never fought or argued. No boy could have asked for a better sister.

With my sister's keen sense of adventure it was inevitable that we would get into trouble. Once when both my parents were working on the second shift at the textile mill, Patsy and I pulled one of our most spectacular stunts.

Mother had supper cooked for us when we got home from school. All we had to do was eat it and wash the dishes. We had strict orders to be in bed by nine p.m., a curfew we never met.

One night we didn't like what mother left for us for supper. We threw it away and decided to fix something on our own. Patsy thought that we should have a slumber party, and cook and eat in her room. She got the electric frying pan going to make fried potatoes and she brought the popcorn popper into the bedroom to heat up some soup. We had the television going as well as the radio. Patsy had taught me to dance, something that our church forbade. We laughed and carried on in wonderful abandon. Suddenly the house went dark. Our electrical appliances had blown several fuses. We didn't know anything about fuses or even where the fuse box was located. We went to bed and waited for judgment day.

Our parents arrived home from work a little after eleven p.m. I couldn't hear everything they said but I knew we were in a heap of trouble.

Our punishment the next day was to spend the whole day outside without the use of anything requiring electricity. We were allowed three bathroom visits but could not turn on the light. We were allowed back in after the sun went down but we were still refused access to anything that need electrical power. Now that I think about it, it was quite a fitting punishment. We misused the electricity and had to go 24 hours without it.

I was glad we didn't screw up the toilet!

We both grew up and my sister found a new hobby: boys. I was jealous of those awkward creatures that came calling for her. I tormented them and tried to drive them away. Some things are more powerful than the antics of a little boy. I had to give up and resign myself to the fact that one of those morons would actually take my sister away.

Patsy fell in love, got married and became the mother of three wonderful children. Ii is hard to believe that she is now a grandmother. When I close my eyes, I still see us at that slumber party, laughing and singing and eating.

I am glad that love, not biology, defines a family. Love is still the strongest force in the universe. It will never die and will outlast all the guns, weapons and evil that men do to each other. Love created a family that included my cousin-sister, Patsy.

This was an example of love in action. When would the whole world learn that lesson?

Castor Oil and Runny Religion

My father was raised in the mountains of North Carolina near North Wilkesboro. He was the fifth child born into a family of seven kids. Their home was L-shaped with a fireplace that opened up on both sides. The shorter part of the L was the kitchen. My grandmother cooked using that fireplace as well as her old wood cook stove.

Father had five brothers and one sister. The boys had to share one bedroom in order to give the only girl her privacy. The fireplace was their only source of heat.

The house was built of rough planks that my grandfather cut and sawed from timber on the land.

They were farmers like everybody else living in those hills. The land was rocky and hard but they survived and enjoyed life.

Twice a year my grandmother declared that everybody needed "cleaning out." According to her, "Your body got sluggish because it was full of bad bugs and if you didn't wash all that mess out of your system you would get sick."

The miracle cure was castor oil. Few people today have heard of castor oil much less tried it. I think it's is still available in drug stores although I can't believe that sales are soaring. It was a nasty tasting concoction that would have caused even Mother Teresa to cuss. But my grandmother swore by this evil liquid medicine and dosed it out regularly to any of her children who complained of any type of stomach ailment.

When the castor oil came out every spring and fall all of the children lined up to take their dose. The day chosen was the first day of spring; the day of daffodils, yellow bells, bluebirds, and castor oil. Everybody lined up according to age from the oldest to the youngest. Grandma would go down the line with a spoon and bottle. You couldn't refuse to take it and there was nowhere to hide. You just had to stand there and take it. Even my grandfather stood in line in this awful ritual.

For those non-southern readers, castor oil is a powerful laxative. It is slick and oily and tastes worse than cat pee. If you take it, don't plan any activity for at least 24 hours after taking a dose. Most of that time will be spent in the bathroom while all the bad junk in your body is being swept away. It works better than a roto-rooter.

Castor oil could be used by the military as a secret weapon. Make our enemies take it. They will be too busy to attack us unless they can do it from a toilet. Oil would not be the only thing flowing in the Middle East.

There was a cold snap in the mountains one spring on castor oil day. It snowed during the night. Early the next morning the snow changed to frozen rain. A thin, slick layer of ice fell on top of that snow. My father awoke at sunup and felt a familiar pain in his stomach. The castor oil had worked its magic. He sailed out of bed, out the front door and made a mad dash for the outhouse, which was at the bottom of the hill near the creek. When his bare feet hit the ground, or rather, the ice, he slipped and slid all the way down the hill and into the creek. After getting up out of that freezing water he looked back the way he came down the hill and saw that as soon as he hit the ice Mother Nature had taken over. The ice was streaked with a dark brown line all the way from the house to the creek.

Snow is a beautiful thing. Norman Rockwell painted lovely scenes of snowdrifts and candle lit cottages. Christmas cards portray lovely pictures of serene beauty as the moon reflects on new fallen snow. Songs are written about snow. Children lie in the snow and make snow angels.

But standing at the bottom of that hill looking at the trail of shame that my dad had deposited on the ice, he knew that this was a story that would follow him forever. His screams had woke up his brothers and they were standing on the porch at the house laughing hysterically. From that moment on my dad was the butt (no pun intended) to all kinds of snow jokes. His new nickname was the snowshit bird.

His brothers never missed an opportunity to tell this story and embarrass my dad. They changed the words of the song; "Over the river and through the woods to grandmother's house we go" to "Over the snow and down the creek our brother's ass did slide. The oil knew the way to carry its prey to the frozen water cold."

If someone had told me I would be including a chapter in my book on laxatives and their results I would not have believed it. But the stories are too funny to ignore, especially the incident involving my college choir.

We were on our spring tour, singing in churches in Tennessee, Alabama, and Missouri. We gave concerts, promoted our college and raised money. I attended a private religious college (That shall remain nameless at their request.). Some colleges have an alumni hall of fame that pays tribute to outstanding graduates.

My alma mater probably has a picture of me with the caption, "Don't let this happen to you."

As I matured I discovered that I liked all the things that they believed were wicked;

alcohol, dancing, movies, sex…you know, all the fun stuff.

Spring choir tour was a busy week. We traveled all day, set up our equipment, rehearsed, ate a meal prepared by the church ladies, and then performed. At night, we paired up to spend the night with church members. They would give us a place to sleep, feed us breakfast and bring us to back to the church the next morning in time to get on the bus. Most nights we would eat at the church before the service.

In Missouri we were the victims of a cruel prank involving laxatives. We got to town early and the church had put together a huge meal for us. Our director preferred for us to eat around four p.m. That way we would not be so full that it affected our singing. The youth group of that church was in charge of the desert table that was filled with all kinds of chocolate desserts; pie, chocolate cake, brownies, fudge, chocolate pudding, chocolate cup cakes and chocolate candy.

Unfortunately, and uncharitably, they had added a secret ingredient that is not normally a part of a chocolate dessert recipe. The secret ingredient was Ex-lax. Ex-lax is a popular laxative packaged in the form of chocolate bars. Every desert prepared by these young people had been saturated with Ex-lax.

41

Extra sugar had been added to hide any sign of bitterness.

I have never really cared a lot for desserts so I didn't have any of the chocolate delights. This proved to be a smart choice. My fellow choir members, however, dived into those deserts as if it was their last meal before being sent to the electric chair.

The service was supposed to begin at seven p.m. We sang for about 40 minutes and while we took a break somebody from the college would give a devotion and a talk promoting our school. After that, the choir would return and sing for about another 30 minutes. That break would give us a chance to change costumes and go to the bathroom. It was during this break that the Ex-lax began to rear its ugly head and several of the choir members complained about pains in their stomach. The director told them to get over it, and get out there and sing.

The first few minutes of the second half went fine, but after ten minutes, I noticed the guy next to me was sweating profusely. The church was not hot so I wondered what was wrong with him. He started to sway and quietly moan, shifting from one foot to the other. The choir director gave him a dirty look but the boy continued to groan and moan. His swaying got more pronounced. I tried get the attention of the director and the boy next to me at the same time when I saw a look of panic come across the face of our director. The whole choir was beginning to have the same symptoms as that boy beside me. Then, right in the middle of a song, the boy bolted off the platform and ran out the back of the church. Another boy, then a girl, then another boy and girl followed him. The choir was dissolving right there on the spot. When the tallest boy in the choir slipped and fell trying to escape, the director turned to the audience, apologized and asked the minister to close the service. We all rushed out and downstairs to see what was wrong with our fellow choir members. It was a pitiful sight. The bathrooms were all full and people were standing outside begging for a vacant toilet. There was no time for modesty. As soon as a stall became empty someone rushed in and let the Ex-lax do its thing.

We survived the ordeal and we were told afterwards that the young people had confessed to the Ex-lax prank. They had apologized and seemed sincerely sorry.

We were lucky that there were no lasting effects from the Ex-lax. Unless you count the times I cracked up when we sang the hymn, "Flow Through Me."

Super Heroes and Other Myths

I have known only one real super hero. He was my dad. Everybody else pales in comparison. He was always calm in a crisis, level-headed and in control. Some of this was a result of his military training during World War II, but most of it was just him.

I remember once during the Christmas holidays we built a fire in our fireplace. Sometime during the middle of the night, I was awakened by my mother who was in a panic. There was a fault in the fireplace and somehow the hot ashes caught the wooden floor on fire. Still in a daze, I stumbled into the den and saw my dad attacking the wall with an axe. He single-handedly put out the fire before the firemen arrived while my mother and I ran around the house screaming and trying to save our clothes. When the fire truck arrived they found my mother and I standing outside holding giant piles of clothes in our arms and crying hysterically. My dad, on the other hand, was sitting quietly in the den proudly observing his handiwork.

I did not inherit my dad's trait of being calm in a crisis. One night I was helping my mother do the dishes when she took a little bite of cornbread. I was chatting away about a movie I had seen on television when I noticed my mother had bent over and was clutching her throat. I thought she was laughing at my description of this movie so I started to laugh also. Then she straightened up and I realized that she was choking! So, what did I do? I screamed like a bad actress in a low budget horror movie. My dad came running into the room, saw my mother and immediately took action. He grabbed her and suddenly the cornbread flew out of her mouth. He had saved the day once again.

This was followed by a lecture about my inability to remain calm in a crisis. I hated myself.

I am resigned to the fact that I cannot remain calm in these situations because I am not biologically programmed to be calm. I am programmed to scream and yell and run around like an idiot so that somebody else can be a hero. That is my lot in life. I am the one destined to be the butt of the jokes that the onlookers at a crisis can take jabs at. If I had been in charge of the D-Day invasion, we would all be speaking German and eating sauerkraut because I would have been running up and down the beach screaming. Spiderman and Superman are safe in their positions. They have nothing to fear from me.

There was one time that I tried to be a hero but it ended with the usual results. My mother, sister and I were home alone one night. Dad was working the night shift at the mill.

My sister and I were awakened at two a.m. when we heard our mother rambling through the house going from room to room looking out of the windows.

"What's going on?" my sister asked.

"There is a peeping Tom in the neighborhood and I just saw him in our yard," our mother said.

"Oh my God! Call the police!" my sister cried.

"I have," my mother yelled back. "But you know how long it takes them to get here. Look, there he is!"

Sure enough, when we looked out the living room window, we saw the shadowy figure of a man moving slowly towards the back door. I disappeared for a minute and returned to the living room with Dad's rifle in hand. Mother and Patsy had moved to the kitchen and were staring at the back door. We heard him on the steps.

"Okay you low life!" I yelled. "Move away from the door! I have a gun pointed at this door and I'm not afraid to use it!"

I sounded like a bad western movie.

Mother had not noticed the gun until that moment and she nearly fainted.

"What in hell are you doing? Put that gun away before you shoot yourself or one of us."

"Don't worry, Mom, I replied. "I have been on enough coon hunts with Dad to know how to handle a rifle. It's loaded and that guy is toast! Move out of my way."

Mother and Patsy went running through the house yelling at the Peeping Tom, then at me and then at the police who had not yet shown up. In the meantime, I was mentally preparing for the show down at the OK Corral.

When the police pulled into the driveway and knocked on the front door, the noise startled me and I jerked on the trigger shooting a hole in the back door. When the police heard the gunshot they fell to the ground and pulled their weapons. My mother screamed and my sister started to cry. After what seemed an eternity, my mother went to the door and let the police in. You should have heard us trying to explain why I shot a hole in the back door. Of course, the Peeping Tom had long since run off. Of course he was never caught either.

Things calmed down after the police left and we thought about how we would explain the bullet hole in our back door to my father. I tested several explanations on my mother and sister but none of them put the blame anywhere but on me. We decided to say nothing and see how long it would take my father to notice.

It was nearly daylight so my mother made coffee and started breakfast. My dad arrived home a little after seven. He came through the back door, kissed my mother and sister, patted me on the head and sat down to eat. While he was eating he noticed the back door.

"What in God's name is that?" dad asked. It looks like a bullet hole! Who shot the door and why?"

I panicked. "Okay, it was me," I admitted. "I shot a hole in the door when the police came."

"The police? Why did you call the police?"

"To arrest the Peeping Tom. Why else would we call them?"

"Peeping Tom? In our neighborhood?" Looking at my mother, he said, "Explain. Start from the beginning and tell me everything."

As mother replayed the whole thing to Dad, I realized how stupid I looked in this story.

After she finished I got another sermon about staying calm during a crisis.

This ended my attempts to be a super hero. I resigned myself to be the one that the hero has to slap in order to calm them down. I have to tell you that after all these years my cheeks have gotten awfully sore. But that ended my career in the gunfighter business. It's been years since I shot a gun inside the house.

Passed Gas and Lost Loves

My father was born and raised in the mountains in the northwest corner of Wilkes County, North Carolina. At one time Wilkes County was the unofficial moonshine capital of the United States. Many a horse trade or land deal has been settled over a jar of corn whiskey. To this day, everyone there knows someone who has a still or has access to a still and no one ever informs on their neighbor.

Whiskey making in Wilkes County is considered as artistic as painting a portrait or weaving a rug. In my opinion, it should be elevated to folk art status. There could be roadside stands where you can buy apples, vegetables, quilts, jam, and moonshine whiskey. North Wilkesboro could hold a moonshine festival similar to the apple festival where brew craftsmen display their product with pride. The government will never go for this, but we can dream.

Most social activities in the mountains revolved around the church. Corn shucking or a barn-raising were common but not weekly events. Teenagers seeking companionship of the opposite sex had to settle for a revival meeting, a homecoming, or a church supper.

Church suppers were the best. The women would cook and bake all day and spread the food out on a long table or on

51

blankets on the ground. Folks would come and stay all day, eating, singing and listening to preachers. Young people would play games and the teenagers would scope out potential boyfriends or girlfriends and spend the day trying to win them over. Aside from an occasional "disappearing behind the bushes," it was all very wholesome and lots of fun. Not everybody considered a quick trip to the bushes unwholesome unless their parents found out about it.

Corn shuckings were more intimate. The teenagers would sit around a big pile of corn the middle of the floor and shuck it. If you found an ear of Indian corn with multicolored kernels you could kiss your girlfriend. My dad was an expert corn shucker and pretty good at playing Romeo. He would hide his own ear of Indian corn in his back pocket, pull it out every now and then and kiss his girlfriend. Pretty smart. He never told me if anyone caught on to his trick.

My dad's Uncle Hampton loved white lightning (moonshine) more than anything in the world. His face was always the color of a red apple. I don't think I ever saw him walk in a straight line. It's surprising that he didn't live to be 200 years old because all his internal organs had to be preserved in alcohol. Uncle Hampton was a jolly soul who made everybody laugh. I wondered why he never married. I guess being a perpetual drunk was not the best quality in a potential husband. It's not that he didn't try to get a girl but the fair sex repudiated his offers and he failed miserably.

Hampton first felt the pains of young love after a corn shucking party. He was walking with a group of teenagers as they made their way home along the old dirt road that was full of ruts. These ruts turned into mud holes after a rain. As they walked along they started a game of jumping over the mud holes. The object was to see who could jump across the longest mud hole without falling in the mud.

There was a shy, dark-haired beauty in this group named Alice that Hampton had a huge crush on. But he was too shy to ask her for a date. When Alice's turn came to jump over the mud hole she hesitated. When the others dared her to do it, she backed up, took a running start and jumped clear over the mud hole. What happened then changed Hampton's love life, if for only a short while.

When Alice landed on the other side she farted. It was not a quiet girly fart. It was a loud, explosive fart that echoed off the mountains, rustled the leaves on the trees and the legend was that it killed wild irises growing by the side of the road.

Alice was humiliated and put her hands over her face. She started to cry while the others howled with laughter and ran off leaving her. Hampton put his arm around her and told her it was okay. He chose this moment to proclaim his love for her and a beautiful courtship began. They were inseparable for weeks. Hampton would pick wild flowers for her and bring her penny candy that he would put inside a homemade card. Hampton was on top of the world. But, like many great love stories, this one came to a sudden and tragic end. Ironically, it ended the same way it started. Over a fart.

One night Hampton and Alice were walking along the same road where their romance began. Hampton was teasing her and showing off his athletic skills when he slipped and fell. When he landed in the dirt, he farted. He didn't think it was much of a big deal and it wouldn't matter because it was a fart that brought them together. But Alice scolded Hampton severely about it. She ended by saying she would no longer keep company with a man so crude and ill mannered. Hampton could not believe his ears.

When she turned and walked away Hampton yelled, "By God, I got you by a fart, I lost you by a fart, and I don't give a fart about you!"

Did Hampton ever find true love again? The answer to that my friend is, blowing in the wind.

Nickel Cake Remedies

My mother was raised during the Great Depression. She remembers unemployed people wandering from town to town seeking work, homemade clothing passed down from child to child, and the chronic lack of spendable income. Mother's family fared better than most since my grandparents were farmers.

My grandparents always had a garden and an abundance of food. They grew all sorts of vegetables, which my grandmother canned or dried. They had hogs and chickens so there was always country ham, cured side meat, homemade sausage, and fried chicken on the dinner table.

My grandmother was a wonderful cook who was a genius at creating a table full of goodies from a minimum of ingredients. Bread was made fresh every day along with huge biscuits and large, crisp cakes of cornbread. Grits were served with breakfast every morning and the leftovers were poured into a casserole dish to cool and congeal. At supper, she would fry the solidified grits in butter and serve them topped with fresh maple syrup. When they could afford it, a banana was sliced and placed on top of this sweet treat.

In contrast to the city folks, my mother's family always had plenty to eat, although was of humble origin. My mother and uncles were seldom allowed the luxury of processed luncheon meat like bologna because of the cost. "Store bought sandwiches" fascinated them and a school they would trade their country ham biscuits for the city kids' bologna sandwiches. I doubt if there is anybody today who would make such a trade.

Bought toys were something that rich kids had. Mother and my uncles made their own toys and created their own fun. A fresh cut sapling would become a toy gun; slingshots were whittled out of forked sticks. Whistles, airplanes and toy cars were only a few hours work away for a talented whittler. They played ball, tag, hide and seek, cowboys and Indians.

A favorite game they played was church. My mother and the uncles would round up the neighborhood kids and make them sit on buckets, stumps, anything that could be used as a seat. They would get several old crates and put them together to make a stage and pulpit. Mother would sing and the uncles would take turns preaching. There was no lack of a congregation since no one dared not play along.

My uncles had well earned reputations as neighborhood bullies. These church services often ended in fights.

My uncles were enthusiastic preachers. They jumped and down and ran around shouting at the top of their lungs. Once Uncle Jerry was preaching and he leaned too close to the first row, pointing his finger at the sinners when he stuck his finger in his brother Jimmy's eye.

Uncle Jimmy jumped up and exclaimed, "Stick your finger in my eye, will you? You son-of-a-bitch!"

Church ended in a brawl that day

My mother was no slacker when it came to brawling. Grandma said she was feisty from the day she was born and would not back down to anyone no matter how big they were. My grandmother was often at her wits end trying to conquer my mother's strong will.

Mother got into as many fights as her brothers and won them all. Most of her fights resulted from her urge to help the underdog. She could not stand seeing anyone being taken advantage of and would come to their rescue even if it resulted in a fight. She also could not ignore a situation in which someone was being mocked or ridiculed. Her pugnacious reputation was equal to that of her brothers. Many a bully went home with a black eye thanks to my mother.

My grandmother grimaces when she recalls the number times people knocked on her door to report another fight my mother won. Her reputation equaled that of her brothers. You did not mess with the Hooper kids.

Mother's empathy for the underdog stayed with her as long as she lived. When she was a teenager she was walking home from work at the cotton mill when she came upon a big tall woman beating the daylights out of a small short woman. This made my mother mad and she waded into the fray. She pulled the tall woman's hair through holes in a nearby fence and tied it in a knot. Satisfied that she had leveled the playing field, she walked away with a smile while the smaller woman took full advantage of her opponent's predicament.

Anything "store bought" was a big treat for my mother, especially if it was something sweet to eat. Once my grandmother purchased three small nickel cakes and put them in the children's lunches. Mama was so excited that she had a bought nickel cake to eat that she kept taking it out of her lunch bag to look at. She would now be like the rich kids who always brought some fancy wrapped sweet treat for their lunch. As luck would have it, mama rushed out the door and forgot to put her nickel cake back into her lunch bag. She discovered her error right before lunch and she was extremely upset. How could she have been so forgetful? It was a situation that she could not tolerate. She fell to the floor yelling in pain and holding her side. The teacher came running to her to find out what was wrong.

"My side is killing me!" my mother cried. "I'm so sick! Oh, it hurts!"

The teacher tried in vain to get Mother to be quiet. "What can I do to help you?"

"Just let me go home," my mother replied. "I want to be with my mama."

"Are you sure you can walk home? Do you want me to drive you?"

"No! I can make it but I have to leave right now. Ouch, it hurts! Please let me go!"

On the walk home, Mother rehearsed several scenes in her mind. But Grandmother was pretty smart herself and it would take some real acting to convince her. Mother decided to go all out—yell, scream and cry.

As soon as she walked in the door, she started. "Help me! It hurts! Mama! Where are you? Oh, no, I'm sick! I have to get to bed!"

Grandmother came running from the back yard where she was hanging out laundry.

"What in God's name is wrong with you?"

"My side hurts so bad I think I am going to die…!"

"Okay, be quiet and lay down. I'll get you some water and a warm towel to put on your side. Then I'll call the doctor."

This was something my mother had not thought about. The doctor would know that she was faking and there would be no cake if she were found out.

"You know, mama," said Mother; I think the pain is getting better. Don't call the doctor."

"Are you sure, sweetheart? You looked pale when you came home and you were carrying on something fierce. Maybe I should call him just to make sure you are okay."

"No, please don't. You know what I think will help me feel better? I forgot my nickel cake this morning and if you could give it to me now, I think it will help me a lot."

My mother's imaginary illness became a reality when she learned that her father had eaten the cake thinking his daughter didn't want it.

The Eternal Square Peg in the Round Hole

Being the odd man out in both sides of your family has got to take its toll on a person. My father and the men in his family were hunters. Raccoon, opossum, squirrel, rabbit, deer, you name it, they shot it. The men on my mother's side were also hunters but they were also known for their fishing ability.

The men caught it or killed it and the women cleaned it and cooked it and everyone, except me, ate it. Somehow the thought of scarfing down Bambie and Thumper was too much for me to handle. It seemed cannibalistic.

I am somewhat of a hypocrite, however, because I have no problem eating a hamburger or a fried chicken leg. In my defense I would like to state that I imagined those cows and chickens committing suicide or walking into a meat processing plant and falling over dead. In that case, it would be a shame not to put their carcasses to good use.

I do not want to know what goes on in those places. I prefer to remain ignorant of that entire industry and ease my conscience by believing what I choose about the meat I eat. Its one thing to see a hamburger patty and quite another to see the face that hamburger patty was once attached to. But, I digress from my point: I hate hunting and shooting.

61

As a boy, I went with my father and his friends on hunting trips because that is what little boys did with their dads back then. Raccoon ("Coon") hunting was the absolute worst. We hunted 'coon at night; late at night; all night; in the fall and winter; in the cold.

We would leave for these nocturnal adventures about eight p.m. and return sometime before dawn. You had better eat before you left because we never took anything to eat or drink.

The dogs would be turned loose in the woods and we would stand around while the men talked about the different sounds the dogs made. I lacked the dog language skills necessary to understand what the dogs said because they all sounded alike to me.

My dad would say, "Hear that boys? Ole' Blue has picked up a scent. Listen for his bark to become higher the closer he gets to that 'coon."

Ten minutes later my dad would yell, "There it is. He's got one treed."

Then off we went to find the dogs and the 'coon.

I also had no sense of direction in the dark, in the woods. If I had gotten separated from the rest of the hunters, I would have ended up a lead story on the six o'clock news. My dad, however, could follow the sound of the dogs and lead everyone directly to the tree where the dogs would be barking themselves into a frenzy. Way, way up in the top of that tree would be one scared, mad 'coon.

Sometimes one of the men would shoot it out. Other times they would shake it out of the tree so that the dogs could have some "fun." It was pretty vicious. They never let the dogs fight the 'coon for very long because 'coons have sharp claws and have been known to cut off a dog's ear in a fight. My dad said one 'coon could whip five coonhounds in a fair fight. Besides 'Coon dogs were valuable and "good" 'coon dogs sold for hundreds of dollars. You did not want them to get scratched or maimed.

I, on the other hand, could have fallen into a pit, broken my leg, and there would have been no fuss at all. It would have been a terrible inconvenience. On the other hand, if a dog got injured, the men would circle it like a wagon train about to be attacked by Indians.

I could not wear enough warm clothes on these hunts. I would be chilled to the bone after thirty minutes unable to feel my toes. It was a job to keep up with everybody else. I complained a lot but, sadly, though, no one ever paid attention to my whining. I guess Real Men don't get cold. If they do, they would never admit to it. I struggled along behind them thinking how I would love to transport them all to Antarctica just so I could hear them admit they were cold.

The only heat came from the steam generated when you peed. That was no help to me since I discovered during these hunting trips that I was pee shy. Whipping it out and peeing in front of God and everybody else did not seem to bother the others but I was mortified. I would almost go into renal failure because try as I may, I could not pee in front of other men. I was ridiculed because of this phobia; so to stop the teasing; I would turn my back and pretend to pee when someone else was doing the deed. I would sigh in pretend relief when I finished so as not to arouse suspicion. Not peeing in front of others is one thing, but to be caught pretending to pee would have been worse. I would have been abandoned in the woods, a shame and disgrace to the male side of my family.

I never understood my family's male psyche. I thought listening to them talk about hunting dogs, guns, fishing lures, and deer stands was torture. The only thing worse was when they talked about sex. I did not have anything to add on that subject either; at least nothing they wanted to hear. I didn't even know enough to make up something believable. This bothered the men in my family. After all you can live without hunting and fishing but you can't live without sex, or at least their kind of sex. I can assure you that the only one who got any pleasure out of sex with the men in my family were the men. The women were seen as nothing more than a necessity, a depository, so to speak. If their wives did not want to partcipate, a fight would ensue. I had one uncle who would push his wife out of the bed and onto the floor if she didn't put out. I came to understand why many of these women had sour dispositions and looked forlorn and dejected.

My mother, on the other hand, was the exception in that respect. My father might talk a big game in front of the other men, but my mother controlled their sex life. It was her terms only. That really made me admire her far above all those other poor women who existed only to feed the various appetites of their men.

My uncles had lots of children, some even numbering in the dozens. Not so with my mom and dad. On their wedding day my mother announced to my father that she had no intention of becoming a baby factory like the other wives in his family. That would have been a deal breaker with my uncles, but not my dad. It made him love my mother even more.

Mom was beautiful and smart and had a backbone. She rivaled Elizabeth Taylor in beauty. Dad was so deeply in love that he would have agreed to anything. He made a wise decision the way it turned out. My mother had children according to a plan, she was a marvelous cook, she kept an immaculately clean house, she made love to my dad enough to keep him interested, and at 75, she still turn's men's heads when she walks by.

For me, this square peg in a round hole feeling continues. I developed a fondness for fishing. I had sex, but again, sadly, not in excess. I never learned to enjoy hunting. I also did not develop a keen sense of direction in the dark. And damn it, I still cannot pee in front of a herd.

Beware the Wringer Washer

My grandmother had one of the first electric ringer washing machines in our town. It consisted of two tubs that you filled with water, one for washing and one for rinsing. On top were two wooden rollers, called wringers, that turned in opposite directions. Once the clothes were finished washing, you fed them through these rollers and it squeezed most of the water out.

These wringers were very fast and very dangerous. My grandmother warned me on several occasions to be careful around the washer and to never put my fingers close to the wringers.

"They will grab you and before you know it, your whole arm will be flattened like a pancake!"

I had visions of my arms looking like those cartoon characters getting flattened thin as a newspaper when they were run over by a steamroller. I don't know why young boys have this morbid curiosity about the forbidden, but it seems to be bred in us. All I could think about was threading all kinds of stuff through those wringers to see how flat they would be. When my grandmother was busy elsewhere, I had fun flattening flowers, sticks, bubble gum, jelly beans and the occasional slow cricket. But as fate would have it, Grandma caught me one day putting my grandfathers straw gardening hat through the wringers.

"What in the world are you doing? Didn't I tell you over and over to stay away from those wringers? Do you want to go through life with crushed fingers? You would never be able to write, play ball, dress yourself, or play the piano!"

She then sat me down and told me the story of when her mother, my great-grandmother, got her breasts caught in a wringer washer.

"The pain was awful! She screamed and cried so loud that the neighbor's came out to see what was wrong. She had leaned too close while doing the laundry and those wringers grabbed both her breasts and mashed them all the way up to her breastbone. It was a horrible sight. Our closest neighbor ran over and turned off the machine but they had to call my dad in from the field to take that darn thing apart to release her breasts. So, when I tell you to stay away from that thing, I mean it!"

That got my attention. My mind was reeling with graphic pictures of my great-grandmother arched over those wash tubs, her breasts flat as sheets of notebook paper, flapping in the wind, her feet kicking wildly, screaming for help. I did not quite believe this story, but at the time, it would have been a serious mistake to insinuate that my grandmother made it all up. The consequences from that would be worse than anything a wringer washer could do. So, I made the decision to believe the story.

I got to thinking that if a wringer washer accident happened once, it could happen again. Obviously this machine was a death trap and should be recalled and destroyed. I then thought about all the women that I knew. I divided them up according to breast size; small, medium, large, and "you've got to be kidding!" I decided that the ridiculous sized ones had most likely fallen prey to a wringer washer accident. It certainly explained why my great-grandmother had to move her breasts out of the way to buckle her belt.

It did not seem weird to me at the time that I was interested in the female breast simply for scientific reasons while other boys were doing anything they could just to get a peak at one or two.

One Saturday, my mother, sister, and I were uptown for our usual shopping day when a woman passed us on the sidewalk. Apparently the Breast Fairy had blessed her because she had the biggest breasts I had ever seen.

When she passed us I said to my mother, "There goes a woman who has never even gotten close to a wringer washer!"

Having no knowledge of my recent interest in female breasts, my mother asked me to explain what I was talking about. So I told her Grandma's story about the wringer washer attacking my great-grandmother.

She gave me a strange look.

I explained, "You mean you didn't know how great-grandma got her breasts caught in the rollers of the washing machine and that's why they hung so low and flat."

My mother straightened me out regarding that old wives tale.

"Nothing like that ever happened. Your grandmother would make up any old story in order to get a point across to you. Now stop thinking about this and do not bring the subject up again."

"Well, if they didn't get mashed and stretched in the ringer washer, how you explain the fact that they hang so low they look like the trunk of an old elephant?"

"I told you to stop talking about women's breasts! People will think something is wrong with you. Boys your age do not talk about such things."

"Oh, yes they do! You should hear them at school," I replied.

"I forbid you to discuss this any further. Do you understand?" Mother added sternly.

I was left without a logical explanation of why my great grandmother's breasts looked flat. It remains a mystery to this day. Time and the gravity must have some part in their elongated shape but it can't be the only reason.

So, I resigned myself to the fact that women's breasts are a mystery, one of the many mysteries surrounding the female species. Fifty years later the mystery still remains.

74

Hog Ass and Hominy Sandwiches

It is a fact that southerners love to eat. Some may think that our diets include some pretty strange things and they would be right. In the mountains were my father grew up they joke about eating "mountain oysters." For the uninformed, mountain oysters are pig testicles. Tasty sounding, huh? That is only one of the strange things that might grace the table of mountain folks.

Every time we would visited my dad's old home place he would go to the creek and hunt for "branch lettuce," Branch lettuce is a bitter plant that resembles endive. It grows on rocks that line the creek bed in that part of the North Carolina Mountains. Now I never tried mountain oysters but I did eat branch lettuce.

The main staple on Dad's childhood table was pork. They ate every part of the pig except the squeal. They ate everything they could grow, find or catch, or you went hungry. Chestnuts, squirrels, rabbits, poke salad greens, dandelion greens, creesy greens, wild honey, dried and pickled vegetables, and berries of all sorts made up the menu of mountain families. No matter what part of the south you are from, food is an important part of society.

Southern women are wonderful cooks who delight in preparing big meals for Sundays, homecomings, socials, birthday parties, and holidays. Sunday dinner, the noon meal in the "country" South, after church was always a big meal in my family. My mother would die before she would allow us to eat anything other than a full course dinner on Sundays. We had company most Sundays at dinner because my father was fond of inviting people to come home and eat with us. Anybody from the preacher's family to aunts, uncles, cousins, and neighbors could be found eating at our house on Sundays. Mother complained about it, but deep down she loved to show off her cooking skills.

The women in our church were kind souls and great cooks, but they were extremely jealous of each other's cooking. At church dinners I remember my mother smiling ever so slightly when she heard that Miss Annie's pound cake had a "sad streak" or that Miss Bessie burned her chicken and dumplings. The rest of us were the beneficiaries of this unspoken rivalry because they all tried to outdo each other and the result was tables heavily laden with mouth-watering dishes and sinful desserts. It is little wonder than most of the men I knew were overweight.

My mother believed in the power of good food. Good food was the secret to a happy life. She believed that most wars started because the two sides never had any really good southern cooking. One Sunday she announced at the table that if she could get the President of the United States and the President of Russia together at her table for a meal of fried chicken, mashed potatoes and gravy, homemade biscuits, green beans cooked with fatback, coleslaw and banana pudding, the Cold War would end. She said American and Russian politicians were cranky because they never got anything good to eat.

If we were sad, she cooked, if we were sick, she cooked, if somebody died, she cooked. How my sister and I managed to grow up without weighing 500 pounds is beyond me.

Mother was in charge of the food committee at church. When there was a death in the family of a church member, she went into action. She called all her friends and they put together a menu. She was usually the one who collected the food and delivered it to the grieving family's home. Only in the South could somebody in your family die and the rest of the family gain ten pounds before they buried the body.

I thought I had heard of all the strange foods in the south until one day my partner Melvin announced that he was going into the kitchen to make himself a hog ass and hominy sandwich. Now, I knew what a hog's ass was and I knew what hominy was. Without going into too much detail, ham comes from the area of the hog close to its behind. Hominy is corn kernels which have been soaked in lye water causing them to swell. When they are dried the kernels are ground into grits. Putting a hog's ass and hominy together was a bit farfetched. It turns out that a hog ass and hominy sandwich is peanut butter and syrup mixed together and spread on white loaf bread. When I asked Melvin where the name came from, he said he made it up one day when trying to find a snack for his little girl.

On one occasion when I was a child, we got a new pastor at our church. The women took turns cooking Sunday dinner for his family to give his wife a chance to set up her household and allow church members to get to know them. When my mother's turn came, she got up early to start cooking and right off the bat things went awry. I heard her in the kitchen fussing and murmuring about her old worn out stove and the fact that only a magician could produce a good meal using that stove. She got so flustered that she didn't go to church that morning. She sent us off and stayed home to finish her meal.

After the service, my dad, my sister, and I arrived home to find the table set and the meal cooking away on the stove. Mother had composed herself and had put on her Sunday clothes. The new pastor and his family were en route to our house.

Mother set the food on the table. She checked every little detail to make sure all was perfect. The last thing to be carried to the table was heaping platter of fried chicken. Halfway to the table she slipped and the whole platter of chicken slid off and fell to the floor. She knelt down and quickly picked the chicken up and placed it back on the platter and on the table.

"Not one word from any of you about this chicken accident," she warned. "What they don't know won't hurt them. My floor has no dirt on it at all because I mopped yesterday. Anyway, so what if there is a tiny speck of dirt on a piece of chicken, people are supposed to eat a certain amount of dirt in their lifetime. So what if I am serving the preacher chicken off the floor? After all it isn't a sin. Now remember, not one single word!"

About that time the preacher and his family pulled into our driveway and headed for the front door. My dad greeted them and after a few minutes of polite conversation, we sat down to eat. It seemed that no harm had been done and we were going to pull off this meal without a hitch. That is until my mother went around the table pouring the ice tea. She forgot to put the lid on the pitcher tight enough and ended up spilling a half-gallon of tea right into the new preacher's lap. The look of panic on my mother's face was unforgettable.

Wanting to help her, I blurted out, "Well, this takes the pressure off of us serving them chicken that we picked up off the floor!"

For some reason my mother was removed from the food committee and we were never asked to feed a preacher again.

See the USA in a Chevrolet

Vacations with my family were recipes for disaster. In our little town, where almost everyone worked at the local textile mill, the week of July 4th was designated as vacation week. The mill shut down and most people headed for Myrtle Beach, South Carolina. Everybody except us, that is.

Several weeks prior to July 4th my paternal grandmother would begin her yearly slide towards deaths' door. She would become ill about the time July 4th approached. She wasn't really sick. It was an act to get her children to cancel their plans for leaving town.

My father was the child who changed his plans. His brothers and sisters simply ignored her. My father was born with all the guilt sensors that his siblings did not have.

Every year he would say, "What if she isn't faking and she really did die while we were at the beach? I could never forgive myself."

It was puzzling to me why my aunts and uncles could live it up during that week while we were stuck at home listening to my grandmother moan and groan. I had to share my bedroom with her and all night long she made these god-awful noises that sounded like a bad ghost imitation. If I ignored her, she would groan louder until my dad came into my room to see what was wrong.

He would say to me, "Didn't you hear your grandmother moaning in pain? What's wrong with you?"

After about three nights of this torture, I moved to the couch in the living room.

Every year it was the same. Grandmother would keep up this "death in motion and groaning" until it was time for her other children to return home. Then she would go home.

One night I woke up and Grandma was missing. I went through the house looking for her, scared that she might have actually died and I would be sent straight to hell for not believing her. She was raiding the refrigerator, stuffing meatloaf into her mouth, in the middle of the night.

"Well," I said. "It doesn't look to me like you are close to shaking hands with St. Peter tonight. It would be embarrassing to meet him with meatloaf on your breath; a woman in your condition."

She was shocked that I caught her and ran back to the bedroom. Thirty minutes later the moaning and groaning started again, but this time it sounded different. She was really sick this time. The meatloaf had given her heartburn.

She made me wake up my parents and we kept a vigil the rest of the night while she reminded us that she was truly sick.

"I know what all of you think. You see, I am not faking. Well, this time I think I may be dying. I'm just happy that you are all here to comfort me in my final hours."

When the sun rose, the heartburn had gone and she was snoring. We went through the day like zombies, so sleepy that we could hardly function.

Then a miracle happened. One of my uncles asked my grandmother to go on vacation with his family for the week. My family felt like we had been paroled by the governor. We were free to go anywhere we wanted guilt and worry free. My parents made plans for us to spend the week driving around Florida. I had never been so excited.

But our vacation curse returned when my mother's parents invited themselves along on our Florida trip. They had some long lost relatives living in Florida and it would give them a chance to visit and renew acquaintances. We were trading one grandparent for two!

Our car was crowded but the first three days went smooth. We arrived at the home of our distant relatives in Hollywood, Florida on the fourth day.

My family was not keen on staying in other people's homes, especially people they hardly knew. My grandparents, on the other hand, were thrilled to be getting free room and board.

I vividly remember the huge ranch style house and enormous yard, landscaped to perfection when we drove up their driveway. Oh my god, these people are rich! I quickly had an attitude adjustment about this whole situation. Their house had ten rooms, a giant swimming pool and a patio filled with every imaginable gadget. They had two giant grills and four tables with umbrellas and an outside bar. These folks were rich!

After meeting our relatives and unloading our suitcases we were told that a big party had been planned for that night in our honor.

"There will be lots of food and drink and lots of interesting people," they told us.

My parents and grandparents were not what you would call "party people." Their idea of a wild night was to stay up past ten o'clock and eat too much popcorn before going to bed.

When this party started we discovered that our relatives lived in another world. People were *drinking* and *dancing*. Our relatives had a big stereo system beside their pool and the music was so loud you had to yell to be heard. Men and women were wearing bathing suits *after* six p.m. My mother said some of the women's bathing suits didn't contain enough cotton to make a Q-tip. Here we were—in Florida—at a party thrown in our honor—with people *drinking* and *dancing*.

My parents found a corner as far away from the music as they could and sat down. My grandparents slipped away and went to bed.

I discovered that night that I did not share my family's disapproval of having a little fun. I was in hog heaven, as we say in the South. I had never seen the likes of this except in movies and I loved it. I mingled with the guests pretending that I was an adult, imagining a movie camera filming me as I wandered among the "beautiful people." My lemonade became a martini, although at the time I had no idea what a martini was.

This party became my stage. I tried to copy the guests as they danced. I had never danced in my life but I was pretty good at imitating the others. Now if I could have only found a cigarette I would have been completely ecstatic.

This was an awakening for me. I understood why I felt like a stranger among my relatives. I learned that I was different. I liked this lifestyle. I felt like it was my destiny. It would be a long time before I emerged from my cocoon, but it eventually happened.

The later it got, the louder and wilder the party got and pretty soon people were pushing one another into the pool. My parents grabbed me and dragged me to our room. I was snatched from my new life and thrown back into my dull old life. My parents ordered me not to leave that room until the next day. Then we would escape from this Sodom and Gomorrah.

We packed our bags the next morning and resumed our tour of Florida. I was sad when we drove away but I didn't understand why. It would be years before I could experience that kind of life again. I hated to leave.

As we drove away, waving to our cousins, my mother confessed that when she got up to go to the bathroom during night, there were people sleeping on the hallway floor. As she tiptoed among them she tried not to step on anybody. She had almost made it to the bathroom door when she accidentally stepped on a man's finger and heard it snap! The victim was apparently so drunk that he moaned a little and rolled over but didn't wake up. Mother ran back into the bedroom and laid awake the rest of the night expecting to hear screaming. When we got up the next morning everybody who had been sleeping in the hallway was gone.

To this day, I wonder if that stranger ever figured out how he broke his finger while he was asleep.

After hearing my mother's confession, my grandparents decided that we did not belong in Florida. So we turned around and went back home.

The Florida back roads seemed deserted for an unsophisticated family fleeing the scene of a crime.

When we crossed the state line into Georgia, my mother gave us this warning, "Don't look back. Remember Lot's wife. When she looked back at their sinful home she was turned into a pillar of salt!"

I thought it was inappropriate for a nighttime finger-breaker to be lecturing us on sin. I engaged my mouth before turning on my brain.

I blurted out, "This from a woman who breaks men's fingers in the middle of the night and then hides in her husband's bed."

The distance from Florida to North Carolina was a lot longer with tape over my mouth.

When the Butterfly Becomes an Albatross

You can hardly pass anybody on the street these days without noticing their tattoos. Sometimes I feel like I am the only person in the world who doesn't have one. This is yet another reason to classify me as a dinosaur. Add to the fact that I don't wear earrings; I don't own an iPod, a portable DVD player, a Blackberry, a GPS device, an MP3 player, a PlayStation, or a digital camera.

This makes me a bona-fide member of the old fart's club. Every day the fact is impressed upon me that society is passing me by at such an alarming rate that in a few years I will be nonexistent. Not only a nobody, but a *nothing.* These days we *are* what we *buy.* Or what we tattoo on our skin.

The inner man has gone the way of all old farts.

They say that us old farts are living our "Golden Years." Whoever came up with that phrase had dementia and did not know what in the hell they were talking about. I would not describe arthritis, dim vision, high blood pressure, and an expanding waistline as "golden." After a certain age, our bodies just give up.

I feel bad for women. It's as if their body says, "Look, I held these breasts proudly

89

upright for 50 years. I'm tired and I am letting go. Deal with it."

Us men develop pot bellies and big butts. Our bodies just don't feel the need to hold in that big belly any longer. Men don't look at their butts. Their butts are out of sight and out of mind; behind them.

I was looking in the mirror not too long ago after I had taken a shower and saw that I now have "old man's ass." It is wrinkled and it droops; like candle wax that melted and ran.

People deal with the aging process in two ways. They accept it and go on with their lives, or they try to improve nature with surgery. Since there will probably be surgeries in my future to keep me alive, I have decided to forgo any cosmetic changes. It would be like painting a condemned building. Why tempt fate?

I am a poor gambler and volunteering to be cut on seems like laughing in the devils' face. Plus, I hate that artificial look that people get after too many surgeries. Some of the Hollywood types have had so many face-lifts that the skin on their forehead used to be the skin on their neck. If they keep that up, one day the cheeks on their face might have been the cheeks on their ass when they were young.

You rarely see a really old *looking* person anymore. When I was young, folks looked their age. My grandmothers always looked like all the other grandmothers. They dressed like grandmothers and acted like grandmothers. It was comforting. When I crawled up on my grandparent's laps, I saw in their faces wisdom, care, concern, love disappointment, success, joy, sadness and sometimes pain. The most comforting aspect of this is it was real, as in genuine. We used to call wrinkles character lines. It would have never occurred to these women to get a face lift. Tattoos and body piercings on grandma was out of the question.

They put their families before themselves. Family was their main passion and we were the beneficiaries of their love. This attitude about family devotion has a long history. In the ancient Greek tragedy, *Antigone* (Sophocles) the heroine disobeyed the king's decree on behalf of her *brother*.

Now-a-days a child might be scared to death if they crawled up on grandmas' lap. The tattoo of a devil staring them in the face and the wind whistling through the pierced holes in their bodies would be enough to send any kid into counseling. Can you see the Gothic's that roam around our college campuses as grandparents? The Addams Family would seem like *Leave It to Beaver* in comparison.

One of the things I do for fun is to imagine what some of these tattoos will look like in 30 years. Those lovely little drawings of a heart, a bird, a flower, the sun, the moon, and the stars will not stay in their original shape. As we grow old our skin loosens and stretches Skin under and around tattoos will do the same. That cute, sexy butterfly on those perky bosoms will look like albatross wings when those bosoms drop to the knee caps. It doesn't seem very sexy anymore, huh? Lecherous old farts might look away.

I am reminded of the joke about two old men and women in a nursing home. The women had been trying to get the attention of the men for months without success.

One day they stripped naked and ran by the two old men while they were playing checkers.

When the women dashed by, one of the men glanced up from the checker board and asked, "Did you see that?"

"Yeah."

"What were they wearing?"

"Don't know but it sure needed ironing!"

It Isn't Fair That I Can Grow A Hair There!

I'm a poet and didn't know it.

It is no consolation to me that male pattern baldness is caused by testosterone. Following this thought to its logical conclusion would make some men yearn for a little less testosterone. If I lose any more testosterone I will have to change my name to Sally. Age does a lot of things to you that are pretty distasteful.

One of the worst tricks that age pulls on men is hair loss. Granted, next to most men my age, I still have enough hair to cover most of my head but I see it taking flight on a daily basis. When men are in their twenties and thirties they look good with shaved heads, but when age yanks the hair away, it is not pretty.

You see, along with hair loss comes weird changes in your skin tone. Since old bald-headed men show more skin, there are lots more splotchy and spotty areas for the whole world to see. It is cruel trick that Mother Nature pulls on us.

Another bad thing that happens with age is about the same time the hair on your head falls out, strange-looking hair starts growing in the awkward of places. I call this new hair that sprouts in odd places *novelty hair.*

The other morning I stumbled out of bed and went to the bathroom to see if I looked

93

as bad as I felt. I tried to focus on the image in the mirror but every time I leaned forward, something kept sticking me in the forehead. What in the world can this be? I went to the night stand and got my glasses.

Back at the mirror I discovered the culprit. A long, white, wild hair had grown overnight out of the middle of my forehead like the horn on a unicorn! When I leaned towards the mirror, the hair would be pushed back into my skin. Nothing can ruin your day like finding a giant wild hair in the middle of your face. Grabbing the tweezers I yanked this sucker out in one swift movement. I prayed that this hair would not be replaced with two more.

Plucking and tweezing have become daily grooming habits for me. It takes more time to pull out unwanted hair than to comb the little that is left on my head. I am a plucking, pulling, tweezing, cutting fool in the mornings.

I have this irrational fear of going to work with a novelty hair sticking out of my ear and the college age students in my campus bookstore laughing and sneering at that hair I missed. It is an obsession with me.

If my skin was looked better, I would just shave my whole body. But buying makeup for the skin envelope for two-hundred pounds of flesh would run into considerable money, so for now, I will continue my ritual: shower, shave, brush, tweeze, and pluck.

I am so paranoid over my novelty hair that I worry if my eyesight goes bad I won't be able to see all those annoying little hairs.

I bribed my nieces and nephews to make sure that after I am admitted to the home from which you never leave alive that they will come and pluck me. I want someone with good vision to check me every week and report if these kids are doing their job. If one week goes by that I am un-plucked, I'm taking them out of my will. Forget trips to the mall or bringing me cookies and knitted sweaters. I want to be hair free in my old age. Shower me down, wax me up, put on clean pajamas and I will be in heaven. I hope my mind is still sharp enough at that time so I can make fun of all the wild-hair growing, unibrow, tumble-weed nose old farts that I pass on the way to the dining hall for my prune juice and baby food.

I hear people say all the time, "I really don't mind growing old. I look forward to my golden years."

I am not a member of that club. I hate growing old. Basically, it sucks. Things begin to hurt, swell, expand, contract, give way, dim, creak, sag, wrinkle and fold. You make more noise getting up out of a chair than a pack of hounds running through dry leaves. The temperature is never right; it's either too cold or too hot. Your pulse rate is faster than your driving speed and your blood pressure is so high that you constantly look like you have just come from sunning yourself on the beach.

For over fifty years I went without a single tooth cavity. Now my teeth are crumbling faster than a sand castle in a hurricane. I have had six teeth filled this month.

People wonder if old farts with *novelty hair* have sex in old age. If they do, people want to know, is it still exciting and fulfilling? I am not an expert on this subject. I do know your memories of great sex gets better over time.

My take on this is given the limitations that old age forces on you, sex isn't worth the effort anymore. It takes me all night to do what I used to do all night. It's exhausting to get ready for sex now. Have I plucked everything? Teeth in or out? Age spots covered up? Products ready and at arm's reach? Did I remember to use the unscented Ben Gay? Is the dog in the other room (a cold nose to the butt can ruin a moment)? Glasses on of off (do I want a surprise or have I focused)? By this time I figure, to hell with it.

My dad had perhaps the best view of life and old age. He said that every day he would take the daily newspaper, turn to the obituaries and if his name is not there, it is a good day!

Wild Flowers and Steel Magnolias

Most of the women on both sides of my family are steel magnolias. They are strong-willed, brave, outspoken, and confident. They love their husbands and families and would do anything, legal or illegal, to protect and provide for them. They are a wonderful mixture of sass and grace, kindness and sternness, charm and practicality. Their husbands adore them and allow them to have their steel magnolia moments. In most cases, the husbands even find this trait endearing. Such was the case with my parents. To an outsider it may have appeared that my mom was a force of nature akin to a tornado and my dad the poor object in its path. The truth is that my dad was madly in love with my mother until his dying day. When she was being strong and outspoken made him love her more. He would sit back, smile, and watch her in action when those steel magnolia genes kicked in. When the dust settled he would laugh and say, that's my woman.

Every week during spring and summer my dad would pick wildflowers and bring them home to my mother. She never knew what the flowers would look like, or even if they were actual flowers, but it did not matter. She would put them in a vase and set them on the window seal over her kitchen sink. I was the only one who noticed this and I never mentioned it to them. But that little gesture made a lasting impression on me.

My parents were married almost 50 years and he courted her the whole time. A silly card might appear on the counter addressed to my mom and signed by cartoon characters. I can't tell you how many cards she got from Bugs Bunny. There is nothing like the look in someone's eye when they are in love. He watched my mom busy herself around the house with that look in his eye.

My dad's comic book nickname for my mom was Lulu. When they were first married he took her to the county fair where one of the sideshow attractions was Lulu, The Fat Lady. My mom never weighed more 110 pounds in her life, so as a joke, he started calling her Lulu. Those of us privy to their history understood that only he could get away with calling our mother Lulu.

Their love was like a medicine that healed what ails you. Nothing that life threw at them was too much because they faced everything together. It made the good times better and the bad times easier. Their love seemed to have this rain shower effect on everyone around them. I felt it and their friends felt it. They were a team, each with their own strengths.

When I became an adult I realized that the love shared by my parents was rare. Today half the marriages in the U.S. end in divorce. Divorce was never an option for my parents. For them, divorce was a foreign concept that other people had to deal with.

My dad had a dry sense of humor and he loved telling jokes even at his own expense. Somebody asked him if he ever considered divorce.

He replied, "No. Murder, yes. Divorce, no."

He bragged to his cronies that he ran things around our house: the vacuum cleaner, the washing machine, etc.

At a family reunion I overheard this conversation between my dad and some of his relatives.

"The other night I had Geraldine down on her knees begging!" he said. "She kept saying, 'Come out from under that bed and fight like a man, you coward!'"

My dad was the butt of his own jokes. He never joked about my mom because he respected her too much.

When my dad was diagnosed with terminal cancer my mom was devastated but when she was around him, she was strong and brave and behaved as if everything was all right. The rest of us were unable to do that.

When my mother was not in his presence, she fell apart and wept, with tears from deep within her soul as she contemplated life without her soul mate.

When we were told that Dad's death was imminent she bent over him and said, "Good night sweet darling. Your Lulu loves you. Wait for me. I'll be with you soon."

My dad has been gone for almost ten years. Every time I pass a field of wildflowers I think about that Mason jar on the window sill in my mom's kitchen. She still keeps flowers there but none are as beautiful to her as those picked by my dad. The wildflowers were their special symbol of love.

The divorce rate in this country would fall if more men just took the time to pick some wildflowers for the women they love.

Growing Up Among the Herd

My father was born and raised in the North Carolina Mountains. He had a deep attachment to the land all his life and he was an avid gardener. His second passion was raising cattle which he did as a hobby in partnership with the farmer who lived behind us.

After he retired, dad bought his brother's and sister's share of their old home place in the mountains. He fenced it in and filled it with cows. He bought a second-hand mobile home and built a large room onto the front of it. Every Friday he hopped into his pickup and headed for the mountains to tend to his cows.

My mom was still working at the time so she could only go with him occasionally. Dad was as happy as a lark up there in the mountains. It was as if he could read the minds of those cows. His cows read his mind too. They knew his voice, his walk, and his schedule.

I inherited a little of his empathy for cows. When I was growing up dad had cows in the farmer's pasture that joined the rear of our property. During the summer months, I spent hours with those cows. I would follow them around, pull honeysuckle vines down for them to eat, and just hung out with them.

Cows lay in the shade in the heat of the day to chew their cud. My favorite cow was so accustomed to me that I could lie down beside her, put my head on her shoulder and drift right off to sleep. She wouldn't move until I woke up. The rest of the herd get be up and be grazing again, but she stayed perfectly still while I slept. I spent so much time with the cows that my parents worried about me.

"It isn't normal for a boy to spend all day, every day, with a bunch of cows," my mom said.

"He ought to be playing with other kids his age, human kids," Dad agreed. "The neighbors will think he's weird. They're probably already calling him calf-boy or something."

In spite my parent's concerns, I continued my carefree summer days among the herd. It never occured to me that dad was raising these cows anything but to be my playmates.

Then fall arrived and one day he announced that he was loading our cows on a truck and taking them a cattle auction to sell them.

"Why?" I cried. "Why are you getting rid of them?

"That's why we raise cattle, son, you raise them, you fatten them, then you sell them for a profit."

"But these cows are my friends. This is not right! What will happen to them?"

"Well," my dad replied laconically. "They might be sold to a farmer or they might be sold to a meat processing plant."

"Oh my God!" I exclaimed. "You mean my cows might end up as somebody's hamburger?"

My dad went outside and started to get things ready to transport my cows to the auction. Naturally, I proceeded to create a scene, weeping and screaming, "Murderer! Cow Killer!"

I played the whole thing as if it was a Greek tragedy. I ran to the pasture. Along the path from the farmer's house to the pasture was a series of fenced dog lots. The farmer was an avid coon and fox hunter and he kept about a dozen very expensive hunting dogs in those lots. Each lot was about thirty feet long and twenty feet wide. Growing on the back side of each pen were tall shade trees, perfect for little boys to climb. In my desperation to save my cows, I climbed one of those trees and hid from my dad. I figured my parents would get so worried about me that they would forget this nonsense about selling our cows. I said I was dramatic. I didn't say I was smart.

I climbed higher than I ever had up the tallest tree, and perched up there among the leaves. My plan would have worked if the tree limb hadn't broken. I fell head first into a dog lot. I was knocked unconscious. I laid there for hours before I woke up with a big knot on the top of my head.

This dog lot was latched from the outside and I couldn't get the gate opened. I yelled and yelled but the dog lots were on the opposite side of the pasture from our house, nobody one heard me.

My dad thought I was off pouting somewhere and loaded the cows by himself and went off to the sale.

I was still missing when my dad returned. The search began. I had given up on yelling and sat on top of the doge house to wait. About dark I heard my dad calling me. After he freed me from the dog lot he was about to pronounce my punishment when he noticed my mushroom-shaped knot. We trotted back to our house quick so that my mom could check out this giant gourd-like thing on my head. Mom almost fainted when she saw it. She grabbed me and away to the emergency room we went.

As it turned out, it was nothing serious, just a bad bump. Driving home from the hospital I remembered the cows.

"Where are my cows?" I asked.

"Your father took them to the sale."

"My favorite cow?" I asked in a trembling voice.

Mom smiled, "No, Danny. Your father left your cow friend in the pasture."

When we got home my favorite cow was standing at the fence waiting for me. Dad didn't have the heart to sell her.

I heard him tell mom, "This will be the first cow to die of old age."

Signs and Wonders at the General Store

I grew up in a house that stood beside my grandparent's general store. It was a typical small town store that sold staple groceries, soft drinks, candy, household cleaning supplies and tobacco products. It was heated by a coal stove that was later replaced by an oil heater.

Two rocking chairs and several straight back chairs sat around the heater. They were usually occupied by friends and neighbors who dropped by the store to visit. This sounds like something out of the Andy Griffith Show but it was during the 1950s and 60s and our little town had several stores like my granddad's, all spaced in walking distance from each other.

I spent a lot of my childhood in that store. My grandparents gave me empty cardboard boxes play with and I spent hours playing with them.

I also got quite an education in the way adults behaved while I listened to their conversations around the pot-bellied stove. It is little wonder that I got some facts confused since much of their conversations would be in code, especially if they were gossiping.

I went home one day and told my mother that somebody in town had given birth to a baby with a turtle shell on its back because when it's mother was pregnant she pushed a turtle into a bonfire and this was her punishment from God.

My mother was upset that I had heard such talk and confronted my grandmother. It turned out that I had combined two different stories. One was about childbirth and the child's bedroom had caught on fire because of a faulty outlet and the other had to do with a turtle that kept eating the vegetables out of Mrs. Ward's garden! Mrs. Ward was convinced that God was punishing her for telling the preacher she wasn't in church last Sunday because her dandruff was acting up.

I listened more carefully after that.

Some things that happened in the store were so weird that there was no way I would ever confuse the facts. For example, one day the neighborhood drunk, named Luke, came into the store and bought all the Mennen aftershave lotion in the store. I thought it strange that one man needed twelve bottles of aftershave.

My grandmother thought so too because she asked the man, "Are you doing your Christmas shopping early?"

He looked at us through bloodshot eyes and pulled up his shirt sleeves.

"See those cuts and scratches on my arms?" Luke explained, "I was sitting at home watching television and they were showing that rocket that took that man into orbit around the earth. All of a sudden these cuts and scratches broke out all over my arms and legs! It's a warning, I tell you. We ain't meant to travel up there in space."

"But that doesn't explain why you want to buy all this aftershave" my grandmother replied.

"Oh, didn't you know?" he replied. "Mennen aftershave is the best medicine for cuts and scratches. Takes the pain away real quick."

The next day Luke's next door neighbor came into the store and asked my grandmother if she had heard about Luke falling into her beautiful rose bush and mashing it flat

"He was drunk, as usual, and couldn't walk straight if he had to" she reported. "I was washing dishes and saw him coming down the road staggering. The next think I knew he was tilting towards my yard and wham! He fell right into the center of the rose bush my mother planted for me when I got married. That rose bush has survived heat, cold, drought, insect attacks and the occasional swipe of my Oldsmobile but he managed to mash it in one try."

"What a shame," Grandma said sympathetically.

I had to cut it way back in hopes that it will live," the neighbor continued. "I swear that man would drink anything. Yesterday he was walking home chugging down a bottle of after shave!"

The front of the general store had a porch that ran the whole length of the building. There were more chairs on the porch where, when the weather was good, the men would sit when they came to visit. My grandfather always sat in the same place in his chair right next to the door. While the women visited inside the store, the men would tell of tall tales on the outside. I wandered back and forth between the two groups. The men talked about gardens, cars, and hunting dogs. They extolled the attributes of "Ole Blue" or some other appropriately named hound.

To listen to these men talk, their dogs could run for the Senate. They "horse traded" some but after several trades, the dogs often ended up with their original owner.

The women talked about canning, cooking, their children or their favorite soap opera. Soap operas were big in their circle. My grandmother had a little television in the store and she watched "Search for Tomorrow" and "As the World Turns" every day. She ignored customers 12:30 and 2:00. They talked about these characters as if they lived up the street. Since we were never allowed to watch anything else, I became a devotee to those shows. I hate to admit it but I still like soap operas although I seldom get to watch them.

Last week when I was on vacation I was glued to the television between 12:30 and 4:00 watching the CBS soaps. Now I'm back at work having withdrawals. I was so desperate that I actually bought a soap opera magazine yesterday to keep up with the story line. I covered it up like it was pornography. Who ever heard of a man in his 50s buying a magazine devoted to soap operas. I am totally twisted.

If there were no women visiting the store, my grandmother went outside to spar with the men.

My grandmother was also a great gardener with an incredible green thumb. Her flowers were the most beautiful flowers in the whole neighborhood.

She was a faithful disciple of that wonderful publication, *The Farmer's Almanac*. She did all her planting according to the "signs." *The Farmer's Almanac* was full of all sorts of information. It predicted the weather for the whole year. It listed weights and measures and sunrise and sunset times for every day. It had ads for all sorts of miracle cures from baldness to weed chill.

The most important thing in the almanac for my grandmother was the planting signs. They were based upon the signs of the Zodiac and it attributed those signs to portions of the human body as the year progressed.

111

When the sign was in the head or chest it was a good time to plant above ground crops. There were certain times, or signs, that were terrible for planting. If the signs were in the "privates," what you planted would not bloom properly or if it produced fruit, the fruit would stink. As odd as this sounds, the fact remains that my grandmother never had a crop failure of flowers or vegetables for sixty years.

One day my uncle on my father's side was at the store talking with my grandparents. It seems my uncle had just planted some vegetables. My grandmother became alarmed and got out her almanac.

"Oh no," she said. "You have planted in the wrong sign. The signs are in the privates for the next ten days!"

My uncle scratched his chin in thought and said, "Well, that's good because I planted cucumbers. Those suckers should grow to be about a foot long!"

Alas, Sweet Tea, I Knew Thee Well

When I was growing up in the South, asking for a glass of tea at a restaurant meant the server would bring you a big glass of sweet iced tea. If you wanted unsweetened tea you had to ask for it specifically and then they looked at you like you were strange. As for hot tea, forget it. I did not know one single person who drank hot tea and if someone had asked for it they would have been put on the southern most wanted list of weird and dangerous lunatics. Hot tea was the drink of Yankees and Englishmen.

While in college I was on tour with the choir and we sang in Detroit, Michigan. We stayed overnight with various families in the churches where we performed. My choir partner and I were assigned to a very nice family that lived in a row house that bordered on the "wrong" side of town. This in itself was quite an adventure for me. That night after dinner the lady of the house offered us something to drink. I asked for tea and she promptly brought me a cup of steaming hot tea. No sugar, no lemon, no ice; just hot tea. I was shocked. When she asked if I wanted cream I said no to everything and proceeded to take a sip of my cup of tea. It was bitter and scalding hot.

Then I realized just how unworldly I was. There are places in the world that drink hot tea as casually as I drink iced tea, places with exotic names and customs....like Brooklyn or Newark. I decided right then that I wanted to experience all things that have heretofore eluded me in the South.

My journey led me to discover that not all people in the U.S. eat grits. In fact, outside of the South, no one had heard of grits. A girl from New York once asked me what a grit looked like. It took me hours to explain the concept. A former boss from Philadelphia who had moved to my town complained about the abundance of grits at every breakfast restaurant.

"They have no taste of their own," he growled. "If you put butter on them, they taste like butter. If you put salt on them, they taste salty. If you put pepper, they taste like pepper. A food ought to have a distinctive taste of its own!"

The problem with him was that he was tasting grits with his Yankee taste buds and they had not been properly trained to appreciate the smooth delicate taste of grits. He moved to South Dakota where grits would not torment him.

One day, I was sitting with some friends in the dining hall of a college where I worked. A psychology professor from a New England area that was famous for its lobster industry attempted to strike up a conversation. During our little visit the professor turned the talk towards southern cuisine.

Southern food disgusted her and she went into a Yankee tirade about our lack of culinary sophistication.

"Anyone who would eat grits, collard greens and liver pudding obviously has been inbred with their cousins and has deformed palates! That stuff is gross."

This was a challenge that one of my friends could not let pass.

She looked directly at this person and said, "Well, I guess we can't all be as cultured as you. Let me see, you are from up north, right? I guess eating giant bugs that crawl on the bottom of the ocean floor eating whale poop make lots more sense than eating grits."

The northern professor turned as red as the lobster my friend was referring to and left the table. Oddly enough, this professor and I became friends but, for some reason, she never dined with me.

Nan Graham is a wonderful Southern writer who is an expert on sweet tea. According to Nan, the best sweet tea in Wilmington, North Carolina is found at the Chinese restaurant. I thought this was rather odd. What can the Chinese possible know about southern sweet tea? I remembered that the Chinese invented tea and they have been enjoying it for centuries. That sent me on a quest to find the best sweet tea in the town where I work.

It was true! The best sweet tea in Wingate, North Carolina is at the Chinese restaurant. Go figure.

Several years ago I had a visit from my dear friend from Philadelphia, Kathy Grace. She and her sister came to North Carolina to shop for antiques. She called and we arranged to meet for dinner. Melvin and I took them to one of our favorite local restaurants located in a restored pre-Civil War house.

Our town is small but we have four colleges in the city limits. They draw students from all over the country so that during the school year our town is fairly diverse. Our waitress at the restaurant was a college student who had not grown up in the south. Melvin ordered sweet tea but the waitress could not understand him. He tried three times to tell her he wanted sweet tea but to no avail. Finally Kathy, the Philly girl, interpreted for us and managed to get the waitress to understand what sweet tea was.

This restaurant sits exactly one block from the giant monument to our fallen Confederate soldiers. I thought it was the metaphorical equivalent to Sherman's burning of Atlanta to have a Philadelphia girl interpret an order for sweet tea in the shadow of a

Confederate historical site. Melvin was embarrassed. Kathy has probably told this story a thousand times by now.

With everyone trying to be health conscience these days, most restaurants are abandoning the good old soul food that was prevalent in the South. Gone are collard greens cooked in pork fat, tea so sweet it could send you into a coma, fried fat back, pinto beans swimming in ham hock grease, and biscuits made with lard. The so-called experts say these things will kill you. I guess that is why both my grandmothers only lived to be ninety-five years old. Just think how long they might have lived if they had given up all that unhealthy country food!

To us po country folk, one of the pleasures we got came from those wonderful family suppers. We didn't have money to spend on cruises to the Caribbean, luxury weekends at the spa, evenings at the theatre, or trips around the world. Our joy came when our extended families would gather around a table filled with cornbread, collard greens, fried chicken, mashed potatoes and gravy, biscuits, macaroni and cheese, fat back and gallons of sweet tea.

So, as long as I am able to remember those dishes that my mother and grandmother made, I will continue to enjoy all that deadly food which the nutritionists say is sending me to my grave.

Folks will parade by my casket and say, "My, but doesn't he look good?"

What do I care how I look then? I'll be dead!

I would rather them say, "See that extra chin? "

You can blame that on too much sweet tea.

Warm Bricks and Cold Feet

My mother and her two brothers were raised in a four room house in our little mill town. Their house was a simple wood frame house with two bedrooms, a kitchen and a living room. My grandparents had one of the bedrooms and since my mother was the only girl, she got the second bedroom. The brothers had to sleep on the back porch.

The only heat in the house came from a wood burning heater in the living room. This was later replaced by a coal-burning stove.

The back porch was so open to the elements that it could hardly be called a room. The planks were so far apart that if it snowed, the boys would wake up with snow on their beds. They slept under piles of homemade quilts, so heavy that you could not even turn over once you were in place. To provide a little warmth my grandmother would place bricks on the stove and get them steaming hot. She would wrap the bricks in a towel and put them at the boy's feet under the covers. In her mind, if your feet are warm, then you are warm all over.

My grandmother had some sort of "thing" about foot care. You could not go to bed until you had washed your feet. The rest of your body could be filthy nasty but those feet had to be clean. She was constantly worried about the condition of everybody's feet.

"Are you wearing the right kind of shoes?" she would ask. "Not wearing socks will cause your feet to become permanently stained from the shoe leather. Do those shoes have the proper arch support? Shoes with no heels will ruin your arches. If your feet are cold you will catch all sorts of diseases." And so on....

I think that Grandma's foot and shoe hang up was genetic. My mother was obsessed with shoes too. If she wore a different pair of shoes every day for a year, she would not wear all of her shoes. Since we only have two feet, four hundred pairs of shoes seem excessive to me.

To further support my theory that this hang up is genetic, I have also have a thing about shoes. The first thing I notice about a person is their shoes. The most beautiful person in the world is reduced to a thing to be pitied if their shoes look bad. Shoes should be clean, stylish and appropriate for the rest of the outfit. I am sick to death of seeing perfectly lovely people walk around wearing flip-flops while the hems of their pants drag through the dirt collecting germs, grit, chewing gum, spit, and god-knows-what else.

When my mother was growing up during the war it was difficult to feed a shoe fetish because shoes were rationed by the government. You were allowed two pair of shoes a year, one for spring and another for winter. It must have been torture for my mother and grandmother.

To make matters worse, as the war waged on, your two pair of shoes were reduced to one pair. Adding insult to injury was the fact that your one pair of shoes had a wooden sole because leather was needed for the war effort. I cannot imagine my mother clopping around in wooden shoes. I guess having to do without good shoes for so long fueled my mother's obsession with shoes, because once she started earning her own money she bought every pair of shoes she wanted.

My grandmother never got over her love of shoes or her obsession about feet. She did, however, get a little confused. One day I was cajoled into taking her on an all day shopping trip in the mountains. We went into every dress and shoe store in North Wilkesboro, North Carolina. My grandmother tried on dresses, pant suits, and dozens of pairs of shoes. All day long she complained that her feet hurt, a rarity for her. We took extra breaks and sat down as much as possible in order for her to rest her feet but she still fussed about how much they hurt. After five hours of shopping and complaining we sat down on a bench on Main Street to have a soft drink. I went into the drug store to buy some refreshments and as I returned to the bench I saw the reason my grandmother's feet hurt. Her shoes were on the wrong feet. All day long she had tried on all these articles of clothing, often taking off her shoes to do so and then stepping right back into the wrong shoe. We laughed all the way home over her "I Love Lucy" moment.

Since my grandmother passed away, I remember that day and wish that we could do it all over again.

My grandmother not only put warm bricks at the feet of her children on cold winter days, she placed "warm bricks" into our hearts. Her love of life and laughter and the rare ability to laugh at herself made her a queen in my eyes.

Modern families exist in the same house and pass like ships in the night but there are no "warm bricks," no quiet nights of sitting together and talking about life and how absurd and funny it can be, no stories of shoes being worn on the wrong feet or snow covered bedding.

I asked my uncle how in the world they survived sleeping out on that porch in the dead of winter.

He replied, "It never felt cold because of mama's warm bricks."

I know exactly what he meant.

I Hate Touchy-Feely Me

In my professional life, I have had the opportunity to take several of those personality tests, usually in the context of some professional development exercise. The reason we took the tests was to determine how I might better communicate with coworkers and understand why I like or dislike certain things. Those tests must be accurate because every time I take one , the results are the same. I fall within the parameters of the touchy-feely emotional types. Even if I lie the truth comes through and I land in the same category.

One test assigns you a color. In that test, I am an extreme orange. We oranges are dramatic, fun, talkative, sensitive and demonstrative. We talk with our whole bodies and show our emotions all over our faces. We make terrible accountants but wonderful actors. We are fast paced and outgoing. We love to tell stories and have fun. Putting us oranges at a desk to add columns of numbers all day would be sheer torture.

Being an orange means that all of the above mentioned traits are part of my makeup, but at twice the normal level. It is sad that I learned this as an older adult. I grew up around a lot of other orange people and assumed that the whole world was like us. I could have done better at several jobs had I known that oranges and blues (another color on the scale) do not mix well.

Blue people are detailed, organized, serious and logical, stuffy and slow paced. They seldom show emotion and speak in a monotone. Most of my bosses have been blues. They would talk about analyzing sales data while I wanted to talk about where we were going for lunch when the meeting would be over. After all, I firmly believe in "paralysis by analysis" to quote a speaker friend of mine. Too much detail ruins a good martini lunch.

Now that I understand the different personality types and how to spot them, I have learned to adapt my orange behavior to match the other person. Remember, we oranges are great actors. I can act like a blue person for a *short* time. The emphasis here is on "short." It has made working with people less stressful; and to tell you the truth, I would hate to work with a bunch of orange people like myself. Who would be the star? I have this horrible character flaw that pushes me into the spotlight. I know it is despicable, but true. If someone beats me to the spotlight, I compensate by exaggerating every one of their obvious flaws.

It's like that line from the movie, Steel Magnolias. "If you can't say something nice about someone, come sit by me!"

There is one thing about me that I hate. My "forgiveness" attribute is as strong as my "orange" attribute and I forgive everybody for everything. I cannot hold a grudge. I would make a terrible court judge. I can't even hold a grudge against people who have been mean to me or my family over the years. Instead I pretend that they don't exist. I don't hate them or love them. How can you hate or love someone who doesn't exist? News of their deaths has no effect on me because long ago I erased them from my memory. I don't gossip about them, think of them, or worry about them. You're thinking that this is only a form of grudge-holding. Maybe it is but I don't waste any time thinking of them at all, good or bad. Anyway, it works for me and protects my touchy-feely reputation.

Once in a while I have a slight urge to be more detailed and business-like; to dress for success and march into a big New York office and start ordering people around; to fire somebody because they wore white after Labor Day; to command a high salary that I don't deserve; to read the stock reports and understand them; to read the Wall Street Journal all the way from beginning to end.

Who am I trying to fool? Me? If I fired somebody I would feel so bad about it I would send them money to help them over the rough spot. Donald Trump has nothing to fear from me. Wall Street is safe from any stock manipulations that I might attempt. One has to own stock before you can manipulate it, whatever that means.

So I will continue to live as an orange, telling stories and showing my emotions. Maybe one day I will get my wish for a big New York office. *Who am I kidding*? No one applauds your for running an office and you know how I need applause.

Praise the Lord and Pass the Ammunition

I was out shopping last week and passed by our local sporting goods store. Out front was one of those lighted mobile signs that hold the big plastic letters. The sign proudly announced: Guns, knives, stun guns, hunting knives, and tasers. John 3:16 What Would Jesus Do?

Now, I am no theologian and certainly no expert into what Jesus would do but I am pretty sure the He would not shoot me with a stun gun or gut me with a hunting knife. I thought, only in the South would you find a sign selling you a gun and a Bible verse.

I am not sure how it happened but somehow in my section of the South, religion got all mixed up with gun control, hunting, law enforcement, corporal punishment, sex, and alcohol. You can't possibly love Jesus and be against hunting innocent animals for sport.

This is the prevailing attitude. If you dare question the wisdom of giving Junior his first rifle when he turns six then you are hell bound. I fully expect one day to walk into one of my relative's houses and see that they have replaced the pictures of Jesus holding a sweet little lamb with one showing Him skinning a deer. His humble robes would be replaced with camouflage overalls and he would be wearing a John Deer tractor ball cap.

A boy who can't shoot a gun by age 10, or worse, has no desire to shoot a gun is mentally placed into a lower caste. Don't fool yourself; we have a caste system in this country, at least among men. At the top of the southern caste would be the great white hunter. Those hardy souls that brave the cold and wet in order to shoot Bambie. Alongside those, equal in statue, are the fishermen who invest more money in rods, reels, lures, tackle boxes and boats than most third world countries spend on national security. Next are the super athletes who could hunt and fish if they wanted to but have been blessed with the ability to hit a ball or sink a basket. That gives them a pass into the higher caste. They belong to that brotherhood of men who understand that Jesus wants them to hunt, fish, play ball, and ignore their wives.

I have never, nor will I ever belong to the higher caste. I am what they call an untouchable. I could not hit the broad side of a barn with a cannon, much less a rifle. I hate it when animals are killed for sport. Getting up at the crack of dawn in the freezing cold to stalk the ferocious beast is not my idea of a good time. I like to fish but hate the thought of being on the water in a small fishing boat. I like the cane pole, sitting on the bank drinking Pepsi kind of fishing. Sadly, that is not enough to elevate me to the higher caste. I think animal heads mounted on walls is creepy and brings bad karma into your life.

I am the worst ball player on the planet. In elementary school I had a permanent position every day during recess: sitting on the sidelines while each team argued about who had to take me. So, short of a miracle, I will remain an untouchable among my fellow men the rest of my life. I am doomed to sit on the sidelines bemoaning the fact that so many rabbits and squirrels have fallen victim to the hobbies of the higher caste.

On the brighter side, I have developed other talents while sitting on the sidelines. I may not be able to hunt deer but I can use words to make fun of those who do, especially their costumes. It is a costume. A ball player wears a certain costumer a hunter, a dancer, a clown, a doctor, a fisherman, and a cook. Some say uniforms, I say what's the difference? A costume is a costume. Some of them are pretty funny looking. The tools of their trade are pretty funny also. Guns, ammo, portable stools, camouflage hats with ear flaps, long poles with sharp hooks, tackle boxes big enough to hide a body, stands that hook onto the side of a tree, liquid deer urine, pocket knives that can do everything except drive a car, and metal racks attached to their vehicles to haul the carcasses back to the house. Our poor soldiers in Iraq aren't that well equipped.

I have learned to take those costumes and tools and paraphernalia and exaggerate them for my own amusement.

This gives me my right to exist in their world. For every action there is a reaction, right? I am the anti-hunter. The annoying fly that buzzes around the faces of the fishermen; a nuisance but still a part of the routine. Someone makes fun of the Jesus Hunt and Fishing Club. Who better than someone like me to whom fate decreed is a misfit among the hunter elite?

So, for Bambie, Thumper and all the others that have no voice, here I am! Sarcasm is my weapon. That is until the planet becomes so poisoned that we can't eat food grown in the soil. Then you are on your own!

O Happy Day!

My grandmother had a profound impact upon my life while I was growing up. I spent most of my time around her and my grandfather. Her advice and wisdom were part of my education as I grew into adulthood. I was the only grandchild for nine years so I got lots of attention.

My grandfather was a strong man who rarely showed affection or attention to anyone. My grandmother more than made up for that by showering me with love and guidance. At her funeral the family asked that I give the eulogy. I wrote it the day after she died and read it at her graveside.

I thought it appropriate to end my book with this tribute to my grandmother.

During the last few days of Grandma's life, her mind became fixated on one particular hymn, "O Happy Day." For three days and nights she sang this song over and over. The words were confused at times and in the wrong order and near the end they weren't words at all. To be honest, it was nerve-wracking for those who were with her. I told one of the nurses that after three days and nights, it wasn't a Happy Day.

During one of the few times that I was alone with her and holding her hand, she became quiet and still. She turned her head and

131

stared at the upper right hand corner of the room and began to sing. This time, she got the words exactly right as if as if she was reading them from a book.

> *"O Happy Day*
> *When Jesus washed my sins away.*
> *He taught me how to watch and pray*
> *And live rejoicing every day.*
> *O Happy day, O Happy Day,*
> *When Jesus washed my sins away."*

Grandma was ninety-seven years old. Her memory had faded and her body had grown weak and frail. We had long since given up any hope that she would be able to speak coherently much less remember the words to the old hymns she loved in her youth. My mother had told me that several times in the nursing home grandma would break out into song and sing every word perfectly, something I had never witnessed. But on this day, in that hospital room, she sang every word as clear as a bell.

When she finished, she laid her head back on her left shoulder and started to moan. I have never mentioned this to anyone, content to believe that this was "our moment," a memory just for me.

While driving home from the hospital that night it dawned on me what had been going on in that hospital room. Her attempts to sing were not the babblings of a confused mind. She was rehearsing for Heaven's choir.

Her husband had been the musical one in the family. He could play the banjo, guitar, harmonica and piano without reading a single note of music. She knew that he probably didn't even have to audition for Heaven's choir but she wanted to make sure she got a seat. So she rehearsed and chose the song that best described how she felt.

But it was more than that. She was giving us a message of reassurance. "O Happy Day" was a testimony of her faith. She wanted us to know that she was Heaven bound because Jesus really did wash her sins away. What a wonderful gift we have knowing that her place in that great celestial choir is secure and she is singing in a strong and clear voice.

Grandma, this is my message to you. We were concerned in the hospital about your constant singing and tried to get you to be quiet and rest. We were afraid that your to singing would make you weak and make you suffer. But you knew exactly what you were doing. You wanted to take your place with Heaven's choir.

To a stranger, my grandmother was a sick and dying woman. I know that my grandmother was singing her favorite song to the accompaniment of that great choir of singers in the sky, whose beautiful music causes angels to sit with folded wings and listen.

So, Grandma, I say to you today, sing, sing loud and strong. Sing so loud that it bounces off the stars and moon and into our very souls.

"O Happy Day, O Happy Day,
When Jesus washed my sins away."

Other Books Published by Righter

A Wayward Journey of Love and Dreams
France and Italy in the 1950s
Joe Di Bona

4 Women
E. B. Alston

Barefoot Girl
Hilda Silance Corey

Black Soldier of Mercy
Joseph E. Brown

Challenges on the Home Front
The Writer's Group

Daddyhood
Brad Carver

David McGregor's Diary
Ian Fletcher

The Deal of a Lifetime
E. B. Alston

Deliver Us From Evil
E. B. Alston

The Emerald Necklace and Other Stories
E. B. Alston

Half Full or Half Empty
Gussy Knott

Hammer Spade and the Case of the Missing Husband
E. B. Alston

Hammer Spade and the Diamond Smugglers
E. B. Alston

Hammer Spade and the Merchants of Death
E. B. Alston

Hammer Spade and the Ring of Fire
E. B. Alston

Hammer Spade and the Midnight Treader
E. B. Alston

The Historical Architecture of Warsaw North Carolina
Charles F. Ainsley

Immersion
Steven Kornegay

Itsy Rabbit-First Adventure
Mary Noble Jones

Itsy Rabbit-Itsy's Giant Leap
Mary Noble Jones

***Itsy Rabbit-Itsy Meets Someone Smaller Than
Herself***
Mary Noble Jones

Kate's Fan
Elizabeth Silance Ballard

The Kingdom of America
E. B. Alston

The Last Chance Bar and Grille
E. B. Alston

The Last Voyage of the Dan-D
E. B. Alston

Lest the Colors Fade
The Writers' Group

Lossie
Nellie Mae Batson
The Midlife Crisis of Paul Revere
Ian Fletcher

Passages
Gussy Knott

Skeet Apples
Nellie Mae Batson

Swinson
Nellie Mae Batson

Telling It Like It Is
E. B. Alston

Those Whom the Gods Love
E. B. Alston

**Three Letters From Teddy and Other
Stories**
Elizabeth Silance Ballard

Whoopin and Hollerin in Onslow County
Hilda Silance Corey and Elizabeth Silance
Ballard

28775703R00083

Made in the USA
Lexington, KY
05 January 2014